Business english

PARA

DUMMIES™

**Revisado por los editores
de Gestion 2000**

Obra editada en colaboración con Centro Libros PAPF, S.L.U. – España

Edición publicada mediante acuerdo con Wiley Publishing, Inc.
© ...For Dummies y los logos de Wiley Publishing, Inc. son marcas
registradas utilizadas bajo licencia exclusiva de Wiley Publishing, Inc.

© 2012, Centro Libros PAPF, S.L.U.
Grupo Planeta
Avda. Diagonal, 662-664
08034 – Barcelona, España

Reservados todos los derechos

© 2012, Editorial Planeta Mexicana, S.A. de C.V.
Bajo el sello editorial CEAC M.R.
Avenida Presidente Masarik núm. 111, 2o. piso
Colonia Chapultepec Morales
C.P. 11570 México, D. F.
www.editorialplaneta.com.mx

Primera edición impresa en España: febrero de 2012
ISBN: ISBN: 978-84-329-0004-4

Primera edición impresa en México: junio de 2012
ISBN: 978-607-07-1218-0

Impreso en los talleres de Litográfica Ingramex, S.A. de C.V.
Centeno núm. 162, colonia Granjas Esmeralda, México, D.F.
Impreso en México – *Printed in Mexico*

Sumario

• •

Introducción

● ●

*E*l mundo de los negocios es apasionante. Además de un modo muy interesante de ganarte la vida, te ofrece un amplio abanico de oportunidades y desafíos personales, así como la posibilidad de conocer a mucha gente y, seguramente, también la de viajar a otras ciudades y países. Como ves, te brinda muchas cosas, pero también te exige otras.

Entre esas exigencias está la de hacer bien tu trabajo, por supuesto, y esto supone saber negociar: buscar clientes para tu empresa, tratarlos correctamente, presentarles con claridad y con tus mejores técnicas el producto o el servicio que les ofreces, saber convencerlos, pero también saber escucharlos, comprender sus necesidades y facilitar soluciones a sus problemas. También forma parte de tu trabajo saber organizarte y gestionar los recursos (humanos y materiales) de tu empresa (o los tuyos propios), y muchas cosas más que irás aprendiendo a medida que avances en la lectura de este libro.

Pero además hay un elemento totalmente imprescindible para todo aquel que quiera dedicarse a los negocios: saber inglés y, por lo tanto, conocer y dominar toda la jerga particular del mundo empresarial en esta lengua. Por esa razón el contenido de este libro está escrito íntegramente en inglés.

Así pues, no sólo vas a aprender los mejores consejos y técnicas sobre ventas o sobre el trato con los clientes, sino que además lo harás en el idioma internacional de los negocios, el inglés. Puedes estar seguro de que después de leer este libro te habrás convertido en un auténtico o una auténtica *business (wo)man*.

Acerca de este libro

Este libro está dirigido a todas aquellas personas que cumplan los siguientes dos requisitos: primero, querer adentrarse en la "cocina" del mundo de los negocios, conocer detalles sobre gestión, técnicas de venta o de mantenimiento de clientes de una empresa, entre otras muchas cuestiones; y segundo, querer aprender todo esto en inglés, la lengua que van a necesitar para aplicar esos conocimientos.

Muchas de las estrategias y las técnicas que encontrarás en estas páginas pueden ayudarte a rendir mejor como miembro de un equipo de ventas o como gestor de una empresa. Lo que te ofrece este libro es una guía práctica para lograr que tu equipo de ventas o tu empresa obtengan buenos resultados, un buen recurso para afrontar ese gran desafío.

El contenido de este libro se ha elaborado a partir de una serie de entrevistas realizadas a distintos directivos, jefes de ventas y otros profesionales de varias empresas internacionales. Este procedimiento garantiza que la información reflejada esté avalada por el conocimiento y la experiencia de estos expertos.

No es este un manual de capítulos tediosos que tendrás que ir leyendo página a página. *Business english para Dummies* es una experiencia distinta e innovadora. Tú marcarás tu ritmo de aprendizaje leyendo cuanto desees y en el orden que quieras. Recuerda que puedes saltar de un capítulo a otro, o de una sección a otra, y detenerte donde más te interese.

Convenciones usadas en este libro

Con el fin de facilitar la lectura de este libro, se ha establecido la siguiente convención:

✔ Se han marcado con **negrita** y *cursiva* todas aquellas palabras de difícil comprensión o

que pertenecen a la jerga propia del mundo de
los negocios. Podrás consultar su significado
(descrito también en inglés) al final de cada
sección, en el apartado "Palabras para recordar".

Asimismo, y por si hay algún término que no quede del
todo claro, al final del libro encontrarás un pequeño
vocabulario inglés-español que te ayudará
a resolver cualquier duda.

También hemos confeccionado un glosario que además
de aclararte términos, puede servirte para aprender
sinónimos y ampliar tu vocabulario.

La puntuación y la ortografía son parte del idioma, y
como antes o después hay que escribir, es conveniente
prestar atención a esos aspectos y ser consciente de
que igual que las palabras cambian entre idiomas,
las normas y los usos de la puntuación también lo
hacen. Por lo que respecta a la puntuación, el idioma
inglés se rige por varias tradiciones, que, en términos
generales, pueden encuadrarse en dos escuelas: la
estadounidense y la británica. Habida cuenta que el
inglés de los negocios irradia, mayoritariamente, desde
Estados Unidos, en este libro se sigue esa tradición; los
rasgos principales diferentes de la tradición británica
son el uso masivo de la coma y la colocación de comas
y puntos dentro de las comillas y los paréntesis.

Quién eres tú

Para escribir este libro tuvimos que suponer ciertas
cosas acerca de ti y sobre lo que podrías esperar de un
libro titulado *Business english para Dummies*. Estas son
algunas de nuestras hipótesis:

✔ Te dedicas al mundo de los negocios, dominas el
  inglés, y quieres reforzar o ampliar tus conocimientos a partir de la experiencia de los grandes profesionales que nos han ayudado a realizar este libro.

✔ Te dedicas al mundo de los negocios de ámbito
  internacional y, aunque reforzar tus conocimientos nunca viene mal, lo que deseas sobre

todo es potenciar tu nivel de inglés orientado al mundo empresarial.

✔ Aunque dominas el inglés, sabes muy poco sobre negocios. A pesar de eso, te encantaría adentrarte en ese mundo aprendiendo algunos de sus secretos y trucos.

✔ Conoces el título *Coaching para Dummies* y despertó tu curiosidad.

Si te ves reflejado en alguna de estas situaciones, no hay duda: ¡has encontrado el libro perfecto!

Iconos usados en este libro

A lo largo del libro verás unos pequeños iconos en los márgenes. Con ellos pretendemos llamar tu atención de manera especial. Los ponemos en inglés para que te familiarices con el idioma. Significan lo siguiente:

Este icono destaca ideas prácticas y consejos que pueden ayudarte en el mundo de los negocios.

Este icono sirve como recordatorio para que no olvides información importante.

Usamos este icono para alertarte sobre posibles peligros o escollos y para advertirte sobre errores que debes evitar.

Este icono destaca el resultado de la aplicación de la estrategia o de la política empresarial que se esté explicando en ese momento.

¿Y ahora qué?

No tienes por qué leer este libro de principio a fin; léelo a tu gusto. Puedes empezar por el capítulo 1 e ir avanzando o, si lo prefieres, puedes echarle una ojeada al sumario y sumergirte directamente en aquellos capítulos o apartados que más te interesen.

Capítulo 1

Reuniones y negociaciones

. . . .

En este capítulo

► Romper el hielo en una negociación

► Controlar la situación

► Negociar sin miedo

► Cerrar la venta

. . . .

*E*n el mundo de los negocios todo se cuece y se decide en las reuniones: contratos, ventas, cesiones, etc. Un paso en falso (un error de protocolo, una mala interpretación, un titubeo) y todo puede irse al traste. De ahí la gran importancia de saber manejarse bien en este difícil y hostil terreno.

Para dominar bien este complejo universo, para nadar entre tiburones como uno más de ellos, no basta con disponer de una buena oratoria o don de gentes; también se necesita mucha concentración, un buen conocimiento de la comunicación no verbal (gestos y miradas) y, sobre todo, gran perspicacia.

Sumérgete, pues, en el mundo de las reuniones y las negociaciones, ¡y cuidado con los tiburones!

The talk before the talk

While there are customers who come to the point immediately, there are others who can't do so without small talk. *Seize* this opportunity to create a positive atmosphere for the conversation.

Ideally, you could *gather* useful information about your potential customer during this short *introductory* phase. Suitable subjects for small talk are, for example:

✔ The customer's immediate *vicinity*, for example, the company building (location, interesting architecture, art work in the foyer, exhibits, etc.), the customer's office (beautiful view, *furniture and fixtures* that point to the customer's special interests or hobbies).

✔ Positive general remarks about the customer's company, for example, *acknowledging* the special quality image of the products.

✔ The weather, but only if it's really worth mentioning, for example if there are extreme weather and traffic situations such as a storm and high water (the customer may be *affected by it*), etc.

Awkward subjects, such as politics, should *be avoided at all costs*.

See to it that the conversation does *not slip into* the banal. Presume that the customer is rushed for time. To make the *transition* to the actual topic, you could *drop some appropriate cues*. If the customer *responds to them*, get to the point immediately. If he doesn't, it helps to ask specific questions: For example, if your small talk is about the company, you could say, *"Incidentally, how do you …"* or *"By the way, what system are you working with?"*, etc.

If the small talk drifts off *unintentionally*, there is only one way to end it: Forget the small talk and make a fresh start – but this time with the "right" topic.

Palabras para recordar

to seize: to take hold of, to grab hold of, to get hold of

to gather: to collect, to garner, to gain

introductory: preliminary, opening, starting, initial

vicinity: surrounding area, neighbourhood, environs

furniture and fixtures: furnishings and fittings

to acknowledge: to recognise, to show appreciation for, to attach importance to

to be affected by something: to be hit or afflicted by something

awkward: problematic, tricky, difficult, complex

to be avoided at all costs: to be abstained from totally or completely

to not slip into: to not change to, to not go downhill to, to not deteriorate into

transition: change, changeover, move, switch, shift

to drop some appropriate cues: to intersperse some key words

to respond to something: to react in response or acknowledge something

incidentally: by the way, while we're on the subject, before I forget

unintentionally: by accident, accidentally, by chance, involuntarily

Small talk (about something other than the weather)

The weather is a classic small talk subject and is therefore *flogged to death*. But there are still plenty of other *topics* and events to discuss.

"That's some crazy weather today, isn't it?" Sentences like these often *serve as* a *stop-gap* to get a conversation going. However, not every sales representative is always prepared for a suitable small talk topic once he arrives at the customer's office. Carolin Lüdemann from the CoachAcademy in Stuttgart provides some suggestions and *quotes* the most important rules for effective small talk.

✔ Small talk is a door opener and creates a *pleasant* atmosphere for the *ensuing* sales talk. That's why small talk topics are always positive.

✔ Everyone has to be able *to join in* the small talk. If several persons are present during the sales talk, it is important not *to exclude* anyone from the conversation.

✔ Even seemingly harmless topics, such as sports and cars *may be doomed* if one of the persons you are talking to *feels very strongly about* them. Carolin Lüdemann, therefore, suggests to not start the conversation by talking about private *matters* or hobbies but to choose a subject from the professional environment, especially if you don't know the persons you're talking with very well.

✔ Getting into the conversation spontaneously is usually the best *choice* for an *easy-going* start but also *demands* quick reaction. This works by paying close attention to your *surroundings* and by watching if anything has changed at the customer's office building or if there is something striking like an interesting sculpture or an *extension to the building*.

> ✔ Small talk *always moves on the surface*. If the *actual* sales talk develops from it, the small talk has ended, but *there is no clear-cut dividing line*. If it is difficult to make the *transition*, simply *make a "cut"* and *get into* the actual topic.

Palabras para recordar

is flogged to death: is used way too much or too often

topics: subjects, themes, things to talk about

to serve as: to act as, to function as, to do duty as, to do the work of

stopgap: temporary solution or substitute, makeshift, fill-in, last resort

to quote: to cite, to refer to, to mention, to make reference to

pleasant: friendly, nice, enjoyable, pleasurable, pleasing

ensuing: following, subsequent, resulting, succeeding, later

to join in: to participate in, to take part in, to contribute to, to partake in

to exclude: to leave out, to keep out, to bar, to shut out

may be doomed: could be disaster-prone, ill-fated, or ruined

to feel very strongly about something: to get quite emotional, passionate, or fanatical over something

matters: affairs, issues, situations, circumstances, occurrences

choice: option, alternative, possibility, solution, answer, way out, pick

easy-going: relaxed, laidback, informal, casual

to demand: to require, to call for, to necessitate, to involve, to need

(continúa)

Continuación

surroundings: environs, background, setting, backdrop

extension to the building: addition, add-on, supplement, or augmentation to the structure

to always move on the surface: to never go deep, to not be full of meaning

actual: real, concrete, factual, authentic, genuine

there is no clear-cut dividing line: the boundaries are undefined, vague, or non-specific

transition: change, changeover, switch, shift, conversion

to make a cut: to bring to an end, halt, stop, or discontinue (the small talk)

to get into: to start with, to get going with, to commence with, to instigate, to bring about

Identify and skilfully *avoid* embarrassments

With an off-putting conversation opener, sales people can *spoil* potential business even *in the preliminary stage*. That is why it is important to identify the biggest *pitfalls* and avoid them in a confident manner.

A sales representative is a good 15 minutes late for his customer call. But he is certainly not lost for words or an excuse: *"Your visitor parking lot is way too small,"* he explains to the customer upon arrival, *"I had to go three blocks down to find a space."* *"Then next time we can arrange for your very own assigned parking space,"* the customer *replies* sarcastically.

Embarrassing situations like these happen quicker than you think, explains sales trainer Helmut Schwind from Gilching. And **clumsiness** like this is most likely to happen in the difficult phase of starting a conversation. The sales representative **awkwardly** searches for a conversation starter and promptly **lands off the mark**.

"I was in your neighbourhood and just decided to drop by" is a typical example of **putting your foot in your mouth**. The customer **is depreciated** to a **"stopgap"**, where you "just drop by" when there is nothing else to do.

Keeping the necessary distance

Private matters can be embarrassing when they are worded **inexpertly** or when you know your conversation partner only superficially: *"And your wife is well?"* – *"I don't know,"* could be the customer's ironic answer, *"she has been living in the United States for four years."*

You will find yourself on the safe side, however, if you **resort to** information that you have about the customer's company early in the conversation. For example: *"I have studied your new business report. It is **remarkable** how well your business has developed!"*. When opening a conversation in such an **upbeat fashion**, the sales representative can be sure that the customer will **pick up the thread**, *"We are indeed very proud, too, especially because we work in such difficult markets."*

Opening the dialogue

When starting a conversation, it is important to animate the customer so that a **lively** discussion can **commence**. To **facilitate** this, it is wise to word the initial sentences in an open-end fashion, *"I read that* *you are planning to expand to Eastern Europe. Which of the countries do you want to focus on?"*

It is ideal if the sales representative can open a discussion with the customer's favourite topic, says corporate consultant Klaus Spazier from Südbrookmerland near Emden. Which discussion topics the consumer prefers depends on his personality profile. The selling expert differentiates between the following customer types:

✔ The emotional type: You can motivate him with just a few *appreciative* words. The *premise*, however, is that the *praise* is heartfelt and honest.

✔ The *vain* type: He *feels flattered* when the sales representative mentions his *accomplishments*. He also likes to talk about status symbols.

✔ The industry expert: He *comes out of his shell* when you deliver the latest news regarding his field of expertise.

✔ The workaholic: He opens up when you drop a few words about his massive work volume and his major responsibility.

Whichever type of customer you are dealing with, salespeople should always give their dialogue partners *ample* possibilities to talk about their favourite topics. It is advisable, however, to not let this conversation develop into *gossip* about other customers. Sales representatives that *give in to* such behaviour will themselves *gain* a reputation of *not being trustworthy*.

Interposed questions on demand analysis it is advisable to effortlessly *steer* the opening of a conversation towards a demand analysis. An elegant way is to ask specific interposed questions, *"Oh, you are planning to expand your product range – does your existing machinery **suffice** in that case?"* Once the customer has answered all the essential questions, the next phase of the sales talk can begin with the fitting keyword, *"Speaking of production costs, we have a very economical solution that should fit your needs perfectly. Do you know our...?"*

Palabras para recordar

skilfully: competently, expertly, cleverly, capably, efficiently

embarrassment: awkwardness, discomfort, distress, confusion, agitation

to spoil: to ruin, to mess up, to destroy

in the preliminary stage: in the introductory, beginning, or opening phase

pitfall: trap, stumbling block, hazard, peril, danger, difficulty

to reply: to respond, to answer back

clumsiness: awkwardness, ungainliness, ineptness, gaucheness

awkwardly: clumsily, inelegantly, gracelessly, amateurishly

to land off the mark: to be off base or wide of the mark

to put one's foot in one's mouth: to drop a brick, to drop a clanger, to put one's foot in it

is depreciated: is devalued, downgraded, reduced, diminished, or minimised

stopgap: temporary substitute, fill-in, makeshift, last resort

inexpertly: clumsily, ineptly, tactlessly

to resort to: to fall back on, to turn to, to make use of, to bring into play

remarkable: extraordinary, exceptional, outstanding, noteworthy, phenomenal

upbeat fashion: optimistic, positive, confident, or cheerful way

(continúa)

Continuación

to pick up the thread: to develop a thought further, to spin a thought out, to expand on an idea

lively: energetic, animated, enthusiastic, high-spirited, stimulating, exciting, active

to commence: to begin, to start, to get going

to facilitate: to help, to assist, to aid, to advance, to ease

appreciative: grateful, thankful, enthusiastic, supportive, encouraging

premise: idea, precondition, prerequisite

praise: applause, acclaim, approval, acclamation, commendation

vain: conceited, narcissistic, self-admiring, self-important, big-headed

to feel flattered: to feel complimented, pleased, grateful, fawned-upon, or thrilled

accomplishment: talent, skill, gift, achievement, performance, capability

to come out of one's shell: to loosen up, to relax, to become responsive

ample: plenty of, more than enough, enough and to spare

gossip: rumours, idle talk, hearsay, smear campaign

to give in to: to succumb to, to give way to, to go along with

to gain: to obtain, to get, to acquire

to not be trustworthy: to not be reliable, dependable, or honourable

interposed questions: placed-between, interjected, or inserted queries

to steer: to navigate, to guide, to direct

to suffice: to meet the requirements, to be sufficient, to satisfy the demands

Take the "so what?" test

While preparing for your next meeting with a customer, scrutinise your sales arguments by taking the "so what?" test. Examine if the customer may possibly reply "so what?" to one or the other benefit you are intending *to quote*. This answer would mean that the customer doesn't attach any importance to the mentioned benefit. In this case you should *withdraw* the respective argument.

Palabras para recordar

so what: who cares, what difference does it make

to quote: to refer to, to mention, to name, to cite, to make reference to

to withdraw: to remove, to eliminate, to do away with, to get rid of

---

Pay attention to body language

Salespeople, who not only listen to their customers *attentively* but also observe them closely, can tell quite accurately whether they are currently in a positive or negative *mindset.*

Sales representatives are used to conducting many more conversations with their customers face-to-face than on the phone. This works to their advantage: "Only when you are face-to-face with a customer, you can interpret words correctly," explains Xenia Busam, trainer at the CoachAcademy in Stuttgart. "Only in combination with body language can you make sure that you clearly understood *your counterpart.*"

Since most human beings have a natural intuition for body language, we can interpret it correctly in most cases without thinking about it too much. "It is difficult, however, when someone is not speaking and we can only observe them and try to guess, according to their body language, what they are thinking at the moment," says Xenia Busam.

Typical behavioural patterns

This happens to be the case during major presentations, at which a sales representative talks at length to an audience. "When someone leans back in an overly relaxed manner, this indicates that their mind is elsewhere," Xenia Busam explains. On the other hand, taking notes, eye contact with the presenter and a slightly bent-forward upper body all suggest *acute awareness*. If a listener's facial features harden around the mouth and he *squints*, this points toward *disapproval* or *annoyance*. "The mouth and eyes *are a giveaway*," the trainer explains. "Also, if someone avoids eye contact and looks to the side, this is usually a sign of disagreement."

Question your assumption

The most effective way to confirm your assumption during a presentation is to address the listeners directly. "*Judging by your look*, you doubt my *reasoning*?" is a possible approach *to coax someone out of their shell*. "Either he will react surprised – which *disproves* your hypothesis – or your impression will be confirmed," says Xenia Busam.

It is also tough to be sitting across from someone with a "poker face." "People like that aren't playing games," Xenia Busam accentuates. "But they have *mastered the art of* reducing their body language *to a bare minimum*." That is why they *appear aloof* and one *is at a loss* trying to figure out what exactly they are thinking, regardless which expression they put forward.

The best method *to assess* the attitude of such a listener is *to prompt* them to a ovement or reaction, as Xenia Busam recommends: "You can, for instance, hand them a brochure or a sample."

A subtle distinction

Skilled buyers and negotiating partners largely have their body language under control. Yet there is a method *to discern consciously adopted* body language from natural body language. "Natural body language always sets in for just a moment, right before one starts to speak," explains Xenia Busam. "Consciously used body language, however, happens simultaneously to speaking."

Sweat the small stuff

If a salesperson happens to be uncertain about or irritated by the customer's body language, it is wise to pay close attention to small details. "For example, how steady or unsteady is your customer's *gaze*, does he look around much, or does he keep eye contact?," says Xenia Busam. In case a customer's body language makes him come across as not very likeable, the trainer recommends using your own body language in a positive manner to open the other person up. "For example, it *is perceived as trustworthy* to show *the palms of your hands*." *Possibly*, this gesture might spark a positive reaction in your counterpart.

In the trainer's opinion, there is never any danger in *overrating* body language. "One simply cannot overrate body language because it allows for your counterpart's words to be fully understood."

Palabras para recordar

attentively: carefully, alertly, conscientiously

mindset: state of mind, frame of mind, way of thinking

your counterpart: the person across from or facing you

behavioural pattern: mode of conduct

(continúa)

Continuación

acute awareness: keen alertness, attentiveness, responsiveness, or consciousness

to squint: to narrow one's eyes, to look askance

disapproval: displeasure, dislike, dissatisfaction, condemnation

annoyance: irritation, exasperation, frustration, aggravation

to be a giveaway: to be revealing, disclosing, divulging, or betraying

to question one's assumption: to examine one's theory, hypothesis, or guess

judging by your look: guessing, assessing, surmising, or guesstimating by your gaze

reasoning: way of thinking, interpretation, analysis, reckoning

to coax someone out of one's shell: to draw someone out, to induce someone to talk, to put someone at ease

to disprove: to invalidate, to contradict, to negate, to refute, to challenge

to master the art of something: to become proficient, skilled, or adept in something

to a bare minimum: to the smallest, least, or lowest degree

to appear aloof: to seem remote, distant, unapproachable, or detached

to be at a loss: to be at one's wits end, puzzled, perplexed, or bewildered

to assess: to evaluate, to judge, to determine, to appraise

to prompt: to induce, to encourage, to motivate, to impel, to provoke

a subtle distinction: a fine, fine-drawn, slight, minute, or tenuous difference

(continúa)

Continuación

---

skilled: accomplished, experienced, trained, expert, practised

---

to discern: to distinguish, to recognise, to perceive, to detect, to observe

---

consciously adopted: deliberately, intentionally, wilfully, or knowingly assumed

---

to sweat the small stuff: to pay attention to details or fine points

---

gaze: look, stare, gape

---

to be perceived as trustworthy: to be professed, alleged, recognised, or understood as honest

---

the palm of one's hand: the under part of the hand between the fingers and the wrist

---

possibly: perhaps, maybe, for all one knows

---

to overrate: to overestimate, to think too much of, to place too much emphasis on, to attach too much importance to

---

High-profile *but not* pushy

Sales representatives, who ***put pressure on*** their customers and push them to a buying decision, ***attain*** only short-term success, or none at all.

To display a strong presence when dealing with customers is one of the most important success factors for sales representatives. This ***applies especially to*** the acquisition of new customers. *"If you let more than 15 days **elapse** between the initial and the follow-up visit, you're **banned** from the customer's mind,"* explains Michael Weber, Sales Manager Germany for Viessmann, Allendorf.

But showing a strong presence *is often confused with applying* massive pressure. Instead of *being responsive to* the customer's needs and *taking them seriously*, he's pushed to a decision.

The pressure already starts while *scheduling an appointment* over the telephone, emphasises Klaus-J. Fink, a telephone trainer based in Bad Honnef. *"If you push the customer too hard for an appointment, he experiences a feeling comparable to buyer's remorse."* Therefore, providing benefit instead of applying pressure *is the way to go*.

Sales representatives should, on the one hand, give their customers enough freedom so they don't *feel hassled*, and on the other hand *convey* that they're always there for them to advise them competently on all important *issues*.

For example, it may be greatly beneficial to the customer if the sales representative helps him with the *transition to* the new supplier. *"This may include, for example, the sales representative programming the phone numbers of all the important contact persons into the customer's telephone system,"* explains Michael Weber.

Palabras para recordar

high-profile: impressive, imposing, daunting, commanding, arresting

pushy: aggressive, forceful, insistent, hard-line, overambitious

to put pressure on someone: to coerce, bully, intimidate, or harass someone

to attain: to reach, to achieve, to obtain, to gain, to accomplish

to display: to exhibit, to demonstrate

to apply especially to: to be particularly valid for or pertinent to

(continúa)

Continuación
to elapse: to pass, to go by, to slip by
to be banned from: to be expelled, barred, or excluded from
to be confused with: to be mixed up with, to be mistaken for
to apply: to use, to exercise, to employ, to administer, to utilise
to be responsive to something: to be open or quick to respond to something
to take something seriously: to not take something frivolously or flippantly
to schedule an appointment: to set a date for a visit, to arrange a meeting
to experience: to go through, to encounter, to become familiar with
comparable to: like, similar to, akin to

Play your trump cards right

While *lavish* product presentations are mostly planned right down to the last detail, salespeople sometimes allow "normal" sales talks *to progress* differently than *desired*. Dramaturgical rules could *be applied* in these situations as well.

Some salespeople are true masters of improvisation. They know how *to convince* customers even in the *trickiest* of situations. Other salespeople get nervous if the presentation *doesn't proceed according to plan*. They need their *firm order of events* to which they can hold on to.

In the experience of sales trainer Josua Fett, owner of Pro Value Consultants in Straubing, the point in time, when the price *is quoted*, *has an impact on*

Use your sales arguments strategically

If you use up all of your best sales arguments at the same time, you are left without a trump card to play. It is more advantageous to use your sales arguments wisely and *enjoy their effect to the fullest*. Here are some tips:

✔ Always cite your sales arguments individually, never bundled.

✔ *Embellish* each argument and take time to present it to the customer *vividly*.

✔ Hold a sales argument back if you're not sure yet whether it is a deciding factor for the customer.

✔ Do not make your sales arguments sound like "counter attacks" to objections, but offer the customer a new point of view or a new aspect that he hadn't thought of before.

the *entire* sales talk and on the behaviour of the customer and salesperson.

Fett emphasises that salespeople who *put discussion of price on the back burner*, are in *the weaker* position and *impair* the presentation's effective dramaturgy. They are *building up tension*, causing strain for both sides throughout the sales talk. Fett, therefore, recommends quoting the price at the beginning. This may even be an advantage in regard to the *ensuing* sales arguments. Now, the salesperson has a chance to demonstrate to the customer, step by step, what great benefits he is getting in return.

Take advantage of each sales argument

Step 1: Before your presentation, collect all the sales arguments that are available to you. Do some brainstorming and write down everything that comes to mind, even seemingly obvious things.

Step 2: Select your sales arguments. The ***objective*** is to find out which argument is most effective at what point. This is done in the following way:

> ✔ ***Subdivide*** your arguments into "***belly*** arguments"/emotional considerations and formal arguments/factual arguments.

> ✔ ***Assign*** the arguments to certain interests, for example cost savings, ***conveniences***, safety, image, etc.

> ✔ Determine what your customers' main interests normally are, for example: Controller = cost savings, production manager = high quality, safety, etc.

Step 3: Now put your sales arguments in a dramaturgical ***order of precedence*** and ***consider*** at what point they will be most effective.

> ✔ The way to start. At the beginning of the sales talk you need sales arguments that ***rouse*** the customer's interest. This is not yet a time for playing your strongest trump cards. Pay close attention to how the customer ***responds to*** your initial arguments.

> ✔ Create positive tension. Once you've roused the customer's interest, you need sales arguments which create positive tension. The goal is to increase the customer's ***desire*** to own the product or solution.

> ✔ The critical stage. In order to generate a real buying need, you have to cite your most powerful argument. Above all, it has ***to outshine*** the competition.

> ✔ Dealing with objections. Once you ***have succeeded in making the customer's buying need reach its peak***, objections usually follow before he makes the final decision. You have to prepare yourself extremely well for this situation: Even if each customer doesn't come up with the same objection, you still need to have your counter arguments ready. Of course,

you use those only if the customer really makes the objection.

✔ Finale. Now you need to play one more trump card in order to convince the customer completely. Which of the trump cards is the most effective *depends on* what type of customer you're dealing with and what function he holds. In any case, you need powerful facts, meaning an effective factual argument because the customer wants to be sure of making the right decision also on a rational level.

Palabras para recordar

lavish: elaborate, involved, highly structured, complex, extravagant

to progress: to develop, to advance, to proceed, to move forwards

desired: wanted, looked - for, required, wished for, needed

to be applied: to be used, utilised, put into practise, or brought into play

to convince: to persuade, to win over, to influence, to bring around

trickiest: most complicated, problematic, awkward, difficult, precarious

to not proceed according to plan: to not continue in line with the strategy

firm order of events: definite or fixed sequence on how to proceed

is quoted: is cited, given, or named

to have an impact on something: to influence or affect something, to have a bearing on something

entire: whole, complete, total

to put discussion of price on the backburner: to not talk about the costs right away

the weaker: the less effective or powerful

(continúa)

Continuación

to impair: to damage, to harm, to spoil, to diminish, to mar

to build up tension: to create stress, nervousness, or apprehensiveness

ensuing: following, subsequent, resultant

to subdivide: to classify, to sort, to arrange, to order, to categorise

belly: instinctive, innate, gut

to assign: to allot, to apportion, to allocate, to distribute

conveniences: comfort, amenities

order of precedence: sequence or classification of priority

to consider: to think about, to contemplate, to weigh up, to take into account

to rouse: to stir up, to incite, to awaken, to provoke, to evoke

to respond to: to react or act in response to

desire: wish, want, inclination, fancy

to outshine: to outdo, to surpass, to put in the shade, to tower above

to have succeeded: to have been successful or victorious

in making something reach its peak: in causing something to arrive at or get to its highest point

to depend on: to hinge on, to be subject to or determined by

to enjoy their effect to the fullest: to savour or relish their results thoroughly

to embellish: to embroider, to decorate, to adorn, to enhance, to enrich

vividly: graphically, clearly, lively

objective: point, goal, idea, purpose, intention, aim, object

Remaining unfazed in the hour of truth

Price **negotiations are regarded as** the most critical moments in customer contact.

This applies just as much to the members of your sales teams as to key account managers.

Even for experienced salespeople, the moment when the price **has to be quoted** and negotiated is a great stress factor. This doesn't have to be the case according to Erich-Norbert Detroy, one of the leading management and sales coaches, because in his experience, the price of a product doesn't matter quite as much as its value. *"How else can you explain the phenomenon that high-priced products are often a step ahead of the low-priced competition?"* asks Detroy and states: *"Although the customer says loudly and clearly 'Only the price matters!' ultimately quite different factors are important."*

The way Detroy sees it, the price is a welcome opportunity to force a salesperson onto the defensive. Therefore, Detroy recommends to your sales team the following **behaviour** for keeping the upper hand in price negotiations:

✔ Enjoy the price talk. A sales representative should stand positively by his product and its price and realise that the price **is fully justified by** the benefit the customer receives. Advantage: The salesperson is keeping the upper hand, he controls the talk. A customer, who had intended **to force down** the price, starts **to totter** on his **preconceived** way **to dismantling it**. Detroy's tip: Start with **well-meaning** negotiation partners because positive initial experiences build up your courage and confidence.

✔ Present the price *as a given*. No salesperson should *tense up* when it's time to quote the price. If a sales representative *exudes* that quoting the price is the most natural thing in the world, he *conveys* price stability to the customer. Aside from the salesperson's inner and outer *calmness* it is important that the price *be naturally imbedded* in a sentence, without artificial pause before and after quoting it. Quote the price in a clear voice, without *mumbling*, haste, or stuttering, and without raising or lowering your voice.

✔ Avoid pauses. One of the biggest mistakes when quoting the price is to make an *emphasising* pause before and after you say it. *"Every artificial pause gives the customer time to think and* *revise* *his tactic. Artificial pauses kill the price"* warns Detroy. *"The rule is: the sentence containing the price has* *to be completely* *rounded."* It is effective *to surround* the price with benefits. For example: *"If you take more than one hundred pieces of this suitcase which* *features* *a very practical* *combination lock, you can have it for 98 euros and also take advantage of the three-month period allowed for payment."*

✔ Select the smallest unit. Large units *imply* large prices which hold danger *to scare* the customer. Instead of quoting the price of 800 euros for a package of a thousand component parts, the salesperson should bring the unit price of 80 cents into play.

✔ Create price combinations. Every customer feels *"revaluated"* if you let him get involved in the price creation, recognising that there is a certain degree of *elbow room* in which he can negotiate. Detroy recommends to salespeople to create product and price bundles for the customer *to "take apart"*. This way the customer is able to create "his" price. *"Experience shows that the customer often buys more from the package than he would buy if we offered him only the naked product at the naked price,"* says Detroy.

Palabras para recordar

to remain unfazed: to stay unflappable, to be in complete control

negotiation: bargaining, discussion

are regarded as: are thought of, viewed, or looked upon as

to have to be quoted: to have to be mentioned, cited, or given

behaviour: actions, manners, ways

to be fully justified by: to be completely acceptable or reasonable because of

to force down: to apply pressure to reduce, lower, or cut

to totter: to be unstable or unsteady

preconceived: predetermined, prearranged, predecided

to dismantle something: to demolish or destroy something

well-meaning: kind, benevolent, caring

as a given: as a matter-of-factness, as a matter-of-course

to tense up: to feel under pressure, nervous, keyed-up, or strained

to exude: to emanate, to display, to radiate, to ooze, to emit

to convey: to communicate, to suggest, to get across, to express

calmness: serenity, tranquillity, quietness

to be naturally imbedded in something: to be a normal part or element of something

mumbling: muttering, murmuring

emphasising: underlining, underscoring, accentuating

to revise: to reconsider, to review

to be completely rounded: to flow naturally and without interruption

(continúa)

Continuación

to surround: to encircle, to enfold, to ring, to gird

to feature: to include, to have

combination lock: security device, safety feature

to imply: to signify, to mean, to indicate

to scare: to alarm, to make nervous, to intimidate, to shock

revaluated: upgraded, more important

elbow room: leeway, room for manoeuvre

to take apart: to disassemble, to take to pieces, to take to bits

Capítulo 2

Trabajo en equipo y gestión

*L*a complejidad existente hoy en día en los negocios hace imprescindible disponer de un buen equipo de trabajo y de una óptima filosofía de gestión para obtener el máximo rendimiento. Sólo así se consigue afrontar nuevos retos, alcanzar grandes objetivos y conseguir los beneficios que hacen posible que una empresa siga adelante.

El trabajo en equipo es un trabajo entre personas y, como tal, requiere mucha mano izquierda por parte de la persona que se encuentra al frente de él, que debe saber manejar los distintos caracteres de los miembros que lo componen. De su gestión dependerá el éxito o el fracaso de sus proyectos y, en última instancia, el éxito o el fracaso de la empresa.

Rules for good teamwork

Together, not against each other: That is the simple *recipe* for successful teamwork between the field sales force and in-house sales.

Collaboration with the field sales force is not always optimal. Misunderstandings, *prejudices* and the **lack of** knowledge about what the other one really has to manage are often named as reasons. The following rules help to improve the climate between the field and the in-house sales force:

✔ Realise that the field sales force **depends on** you. Do not use this "**to put the screws to** them." The more you support the field sales force, the greater you and your **achievements** will be valued and recognised.

✔ **Maintain** an open exchange of information. Aside from the "official" sales meetings, regular semi-private meetings are recommended, for example, on late Friday afternoon. Those help in getting to know each other as individuals and to find out more about the others problems and needs in order to gain a better understanding of each other.

✔ Clarify all questions **pertaining to** organisational structures and put them in writing. That way, there are clear rules that everyone has **to adhere to**: the field sales force knows that there is no **grace period** for handing in the contract lists and that **elaborate** proposals can only be sent out "immediately" as an **exception to the rule**.

✔ Profit from each other's experiences. If particular members of the sales team hold onto their **knowledge for the sake of control**, this will quickly result in in-house power plays that will ultimately play out **at the expense of** the customer. Therefore, enter all new information about customers into the database

and ***confer obligingly*** with the field sales force
about doing the same.

✔ Demonstrate your achievements in an ***assertive***
manner. Some members of the field sales force
have a very self-confident ***demeanour***, which is
often used ***to distract*** from their own insecurity.
Let this neither provoke nor impress you but
instead communicate ***nonchalantly*** on one and
the same level.

Be tough with pricing yet cooperative

The price is not always the main criterion that makes
a customer decide to buy. Make it absolutely clear
that price ***concessions*** are not possible. For this, you
can ***invoke*** a higher authority, for example, the sales
manager. The customer has to know that debating
about the price is absolutely pointless since you are
not allowed ***to divert from it***.

Yet present yourself willing to cooperate:
Make a suggestion to the customer to sort
through the offer once more step by step.
Evaluate every service and whether it is even
necessary for your customer (some services
might not be important to him). This way,

"Together we are stronger than alone"

Could be, but it is not always the case. Teamwork is appropriate
when consensus decisions have to be made or a number of different
skills are needed for the achievement of objectives. For many
tasks, however, it is enough when departments or individuals
cooperate sporadically instead of immediately creating a task
force. When fast decisions are needed, it is seldom ***beneficial*** to
discuss everything within the team. Furthermore, working in a team
can even ***prevent*** innovative solutions. This happens, for example,
when a team member is unable ***to assert*** a revolutionary idea
and everyone else agrees on the ***supposedly*** better compromise
solution.

the customer can have the exact services he desires, at an acceptable price, without you having to give rebates.

Palabras para recordar

recipe: formula, method, procedure

collaboration: teamwork, partnership, group effort, alliance, cooperation

prejudice: bias, narrow-mindedness, discrimination, intolerance, unfairness

lack of: absence of, need of, deficiency in, shortage of, insufficiency in

to depend on someone: to rely on, count on, or bank on someone

to put the screws to someone: to apply pressure or leverage on someone

achievement: accomplishment, capability, performance, activity

to maintain: to cultivate, to foster, to support, to encourage, to promote

pertaining to: affecting, concerning, regarding, relating to, applying to

to adhere to: to stick to, to cling to, to comply with, to hold on to, to observe

grace period: timeframe in which protection is granted, temporary immunity

elaborate: detailed, involved, complex

exception to the rule: exemption from the usual proceedings, exceptional case

knowledge for the sake of control: information withheld by superiors

at the expense of: on account of, at the cost of, at the sacrifice of

(continúa)

Continuación

to confer obligingly: to discuss engagingly or bindingly

assertive: self-assured, self-confident, forward, firm, bold

demeanour: behaviour, conduct, air

to distract: to divert, to turn away, to avert, to sidetrack

nonchalantly: imperturbably, collected, indifferent, casual, insouciant, laid-back

concession: yielding, surrender, adjustment, modification, compromise

to invoke: to bring into play, to quote, to cite, to use, to bring up, to state

to divert from something: to turn away or move away from something

skills: competences, capabilities, abilities

task: assignment, challenge, job

beneficial: conducive, agreeable, helpful

to prevent: to put a stop to, to inhibit

to assert something: to maintain, support, or defend something

supposedly: allegedly, reputedly, theoretically

Communicate visions

Do not just talk about visions but *awaken* them in your employees.

Visionary mission statements are the elementary *fuel* for *entrepreneurial* planning and action. Visions *secure* a *one-of-a-kind* market positioning and build important *gateways* into the future.

But what is **the stuff that dreams are made of**? And in which way can it be realised **purposefully**? What does the word "vision" actually mean? **Sadly**, in everyday practise it is often mixed up with similar and frivolously used **buzzwords**.

Conceptual delineation from correlating terms

For example, the much-quoted corporate philosophy should manifest the management's uppermost core values, while the corporate policy manifests the product and market goals as well as the financial, social, and managerial goals.

The overall concept statement specifies the chief behavioural guidelines and the managerial style of the company. The mission defines the current function and placing in society. Yet, the vision identifies what the company shall represent and create in the future. Visions are the mental images of a prospective reality.

So, a vision is something that looks beyond our momentary existence, it enriches, **nourishes**, and **amplifies** us. A vision, therefore, always outlines the idea of **self-actualisation**.

What effects do visions have?

✔ Lived visions cause an **inciting** effect on employees, because within them their worthwhile future is reflected.

✔ Visions are the source of innovation and promote vitality and a **fast pace**.

✔ And they place the customer and his requirements at centre stage.

So nowadays, it is the management team's most crucial ability to be **masterminds** in fabricating visions. Not to "let run" but to "run yourself" and predetermine what the company will be and do in the future. For example:

✔ The best service in the industry.

✔ Worldwide low-cost leader.

✔ The most successful business.

How can you get those visions off the ground?

A vision can only achieve the desired behaviour when it is communicated and implemented in a goal-oriented manner and when the result is *rewarded properly*.

That is why the managers have *to align these visions with* the individually set goals of the salespeople because *peak performances* can only be the result of self-motivated *endurance* and personal commitment. Your employees should fantasise and "envisage" themselves in the desired condition:

✔ How do you see yourself as a successful salesperson?

✔ How will you *face* your customers?

✔ How will your success *affect* your personality?

✔ What new things will you have learned?

But never forget: No objective in this world, no award, however luxuriant it may be, no promise for a pay raise, however high, could motivate a *mountaineer* to keep climbing the peak again and again *at the hazard* of his own life. Only he himself, only his own free will and endurance can achieve this.

Palabras para recordar

to awaken: to insire, to arouse, to prompt, to ignite

fuel: stimulus, incentive, encouragement

entrepreneurial: corporate, business, company, commercial

to secure: to assure, to ensure, to promise, to give surety to

one-of-a-kind: singular, unrivalled, first tate, first class, supreme

gateway: bridge, link, connection, tie

the stuff that dreams are made of: the things that visions, or imaginings consist of

purposefully: with determination, with, resolve, resolutely, single-mindedly

sadly: unfortunately, unluckily, alas

buzzword: catchphrase, slogan

delineation: separation, demarcation

correlating term: corresponding, related, or associated phrase

to nourish: to encourage, to further, to advance, to promote

to amplify: to strengthen, to augment

self-actualisation: self-realisation, self-fulfillment

inciting: encouraging, stimulating, provoking, arousing, inflaming

fast pace: high rate of progress, tempo, or momentum

mastermind: prime mover, architect, engineer, author, originator

to get something off the ground: to get something going or under way

is rewarded properly: is recompensed or compensated appropriately

(continúa)

Continuación

---

to align something with something: to adjust or modify something to something

---

peak performance: top accomplishment or achievement

---

endurance: staying power, perseverance, tenacity, fortitude, stamina

---

to face someone: to deal with. handle, come to terms with, or meet someone

---

to affect: to influence, to change, to alter

---

mountaineer: rock climber, hiker

---

at the hazard: at the risk, peril, or threat

Recognising *conflict*

It there is ***recurring friction*** between the external and internal sales force or ***resentment*** among colleagues, it is time ***to determine*** the cause and search for solutions.

Matthias F, a sales representative from Cologne, had ***repeatedly felt angry toward*** a difficult colleague from the internal sales force, *"I thought that she's **keeping me on tenterhooks intentionally**. On many occasions, if I needed something from her urgently, I always got the reply 'Can't do it.'"* At some point, the sales manager ***took both colleagues to task***. *"**I was completely flabbergasted** when the colleague from the internal sales force complained about my brusque tone and declared that she's not willing to work hard for someone who **treats** her like that. Besides, I was interrupting her constantly in her work."*

When the sales manager made it clear that he would no longer tolerate this constant ***quarrel*** in his department. Matthias F. and his colleague were forced to come together and search for solutions. *"The actual* *problem was that everyone felt they were put under pressure but were unable **to admit** that to each other."*

Matthias F. and his colleague ***ultimately*** agreed **to proceed** as follows:

- ✔ If time is running short, Matthias F. does not put additional pressure on his colleague but explains to her why and until when he needs something.

- ✔ The internal sales force colleague tells him openly if she's under time pressure and they decide together which task has priority or who could step in as a "helper in need." If necessary, the sales manager is to be informed of the recurring problem.

- ✔ Both sides regularly exchange ideas on how to improve cooperation and how to go about simplifying or ***accelerating*** tasks.

Bringing interests in line

If interests collide, naturally, conflicts develop. For example: You need urgent information from the internal sales force before they leave and it is just about 6 P.M. But you can't reach the internal sales representatives because they've already ***called it a day***.

In this case, it is important to accommodate the interests of both sides. Talk about your problem and ask how best **to resolve the issue**. Perhaps there is a colleague from the internal sales force who is willing to stay, within the framework of **flexible work time**, until 7 P.M. and then start work later in the morning.

Another solution: You try to move your customer visits "***ahead***" or arrange with the customer that you will supply the ***desired*** information the next morning. Perhaps you could also agree with the internal sales representatives on calling them on their cell phone up until a certain time.

Whatever you may decide: A solution can only be found if you ***take into consideration*** the ***varied*** interests ***of all concerned*** and then make arrangements with the persons involved.

✔ Both parties *commit* to be open and honest.
Each tells the other *calmly* and *matter-of-factly*
if there is something that *bothers* him or her.

Since *adhering to* the above guidelines, the
communication between the internal and external
sales force has improved greatly. *"Much of what
caused bad feelings in the past, now **functions**
without a hitch."* Matthias F. *cheerfully* reports.
*"I believe what's most important is that now we really
communicate well with each other!"*

Palabras para recordar

to recognise: to identify, to make out, to spot, to put
the finger on

---

recurring: frequent, constant, repeated

---

friction: hostility, tension, conflict, quarrelling, arguing,
bickering

---

resentment: hard feelings, bitterness, irritation, animosity

---

to determine: to find out, to ascertain, to establish,
to identify

---

repeatedly: frequently, time after time, again and again

---

to feel angry toward: to feel annoyed, irritated or infuriated
toward

---

to keep someone on tenterhooks intentionally: to keep
someone hanging on purpose

---

to take someone to task: to confront, give a talking-to,
rebuke, or reprimand someone

---

to be completely flabbergasted: to be totally stunned
or shocked, to be left speechless

---

to treat: to act or behave towards

---

quarrel: dispute, disagreement, clash, squabble, feud

---

to admit: to confess, to acknowledge, to reveal, to disclose,
to divulge

(continúa)

Continuación

ultimately: in the end, eventually, finally

to proceed: to go on, to carry on, to continue

to accelerate: to step up, to speed up, to quicken, to expedite

to commit: to promise, to vow, to give one's word, to pledge

calmly: quietly, softly, gently

matter-of-factly: factually, straightforwardly

to bother: to trouble, to upset, to concern, to distress, to perturb

to adhere to: to stick to, to abide by, to comply with, to follow

to function without a hitch: to go off smoothly, easily, or effortlessly

cheerfully: happily, joyfully, optimistically

to bring in line: to accommodate, to harmonise

to call it a day: to finish or knock off work

to resolve the issue: to work out or sort out the problem

flexible work time: adaptable working hours, flexitime

ahead: forward, to the front

desired: wanted, needed, required, looked for

to take into consideration: to take into account, to pay regard or heed to

varied: diverse, wide-ranging, miscellaneous, different

of all concerned: of everyone involved or implicated

A perfect team

If **the scheduling of appointments is outsourced** to a call centre, the coordination and communication between sales representative and call centre agent needs to function **smoothly**.

"How in the world can they talk with our customers?" was one of the **initial** reactions from the sales force at Stäubli Tec-Systems Connectors, Bayreuth, when they found out that **future** scheduling of appointments would be outsourced to an external Call Centre, the CommuniCall Contact Center, Bayreuth. *"The sales force's greatest **fear** was **to be cut down** in their freedom to plan,"* reports regional sales manager Andreas Lanßky. However, for managing director Heinz Maisel, these initial reactions were not an **obstacle**. He felt sure that the sales force would quickly profit from the collaboration.

First hurdles taken successfully

The four-week pilot phase, which involved two Stäubli sales representatives, already **proved Heinz Maisel right**. One of the salespeople was Norbert Dörfler. From the beginning, he took a positive view of the project but he also knew that obstacles had to be dealt with in the initial phase. One example was effective route planning. *"When we started out, it sometimes happened that we had to go from one customer to the next who was 70 miles away,"* says Dörfler.

Raising the scheduling quality

A **much greater challenge**, however, was **achieving** a high scheduling quality. *"It is top priority to be as high as possible,"* **emphasises** Andreas Lanßky. For the call centre staff to be in a position to schedule useful appointments, they first had to be trained in product knowledge. **Beyond that**, they receive continuous training from the regional sales managers.

*"We are the **link** between the scheduling centre and the sales force,"* reports Lanßky. To him, smooth communication is what it's all about.

This is also the case for direct collaboration between the call centre agent and sales representative. *"Of course, we discuss with the agents how to best start the call, how to determine the appropriate contact or which questions to ask,"* explains Norbert Dörfler. *"The better the scheduling centre has been **briefed**, the greater the scheduling quality,"* adds Andreas Lanßky. Usually, Norbert Dörfler is very satisfied with the quality: *"The contacts are well informed about the concrete reason for the sales representative's visit and are usually well prepared. In many instances, all other important contacts are present at the first visit."*

Sales force maintains scheduling power

Norbert Dörfler confirms that the sales force still **remains in charge of** scheduling. The central control medium is an internet-based appointment calendar which is used by the sales representative and the call centre agent to enter appointments and **leads**. *"The call centre only schedules appointments for the time-periods we **release** on the calendar,"* reports Norbert Dörfler. *"If I mark an office day, the agent knows not to schedule any appointments for that day."* Also, the sales representatives take care of their most important

---

Everyone has to do their share

Even one year after **completion** of the pilot phase, all involved work on **continuous** improvement. The agents receive further training from Stäubli's regional sales managers. Once a week, they get feedback about the appointments they scheduled. "This system lives from ideas," says Andreas Lanßky. "***It's key*** that everyone is **backing** it 100%."

customers themselves. "*The call centre agent only schedules appointments for the released times with new customers or B and C customers,*" says Dörfler.

Conclusion: It already became clear during the pilot phase that this new procedure made life significantly easier for the sales force. Sales representatives are able to make more visits than before and the visit's efficiency has clearly increased.

Palabras para recordar

the scheduling of appointments: the setting up or arrangement of a meeting

to be outsourced: to be subcontracted, contracted out, or delegated

smoothly: without a hitch, well, efficiently, slickly, effortlessly, easily

initial: first, early, preliminary

future: upcoming, forthcoming, expected, yet to come

fear: worry, concern, misgiving, unease, dread

to be cut down: to be limited, constrained, reduced, or restricted

obstacle: hindrance, complication, problem, hurdle

to prove someone right: to show that someone is absolutely correct

to raise: to increase, to improve, to advance, to augment

much greater challenge: much more difficult task or venture

to achieve: to attain, to reach, to arrive at, to realise, to get

to emphasise: to highlight, to stress, to underline, to accentuate

beyond that: above that, in addition to that, outside of that, over and above that

(continúa)

Continuación

---

link: connection, tie, bond

---

to brief: to inform, to prepare, to instruct, to fill in, to update, to advise

---

to maintain: to keep, to retain, to uphold, to sustain

---

to remain in charge of: to stay in control or in command of

---

lead: information, pointer, tip, suggestion

---

to release: to give the green light to, to make available

---

to do one's share: to do one's bit, to play one's part, to pitch in, to cooperate, to lend a hand

---

completion: close, conclusion, finish, ending, finalisation

---

continuous: non-stop, constant, perpetual, uninterrupted

---

to be key: to be important, crucial, vital, or critical

---

to back something: to stand by, side with, support, or endorse something

---

Selling successfully as a team

The times of the *lone fighters* are *passé*. Nowadays, *elaborate* business development projects are increasingly handled per "team selling."

Selling products as a team? For a medium-sized mechanical engineering company, located in Nürtingen, this marketing policy has *been common practise* for years. It has always been customary there, for service technicians *to serve as an extension of* the field sales force, to inform their contacts in the customer companies about new product solutions and report back to the sales department when they *detect* new requirements. The designing and production engineers *accompany* the sales

representatives when the customer needs
special solutions.

Such a good example always **sets a precedent**. That
is why this strategy, namely "team selling," is steadily
finding followers in other industries as well. For
example, in the consumer goods industry:

There, the key account manager brings along
colleagues from the marketing department to the
annual appraisals, where plans are made with a
customer for **conjoint** advertising or promotional
campaigns. And when important customers in
financial sales want to be consulted on how
to pocket the highest profits for their money, the
account manager may just seek help from his bank's
investment experts. "*The future belongs to multiteam-
selling,*" two corporate consultants from Hildesheim,
Dr. Albert Siepe and Henner Lenfers, explain.

Multifaceted variations possible

On the basis of the business development tasks,
the members of the selling team are **assembled**.
In everyday sales practise, the following variants
have become apparent:

The members of the field sales force and the
customer service associates are acting together
when established customers need to be cared for.
Members of the field sales force and telemarketers
are merging as a team when orders **are solicited**
from the B and C customers. Key account managers
and product experts are forming a team when
special solutions are created for key accounts.
Customer service is turning into an extension of
the sales department to observe when replacement
purchases are due for the customer. The sales
department, in turn, is reporting to customer service
when services are to be sold along with the product.

Palabras para recordar

lone fighter: solary, companionless, unaccompanied, or single combatant

elaborate: complex, detailed, involved, painstaking, complicated

to be common practise: to be everyday, routine, or standard procedure

to serve as an extension of something: to function or act as an addition or adjunct to something

to detect: to notice, to identify, to recognise, to distinguish, to become aware of

to accompany: to go together with, to go along with, to come with

to set a precedent: to become the standard or guide

annual appraisals: yearly assessments, evaluations, reviews, negotiations, or talks

conjoint: shared, combined, concerted

to pocket: to rake in, to gather in, to earn, to pull in, to accumulate

multifaceted: varied, manifold, diverse

to assemble: to bring together, to put together, to round up, to collect

are merging as: are coming together, joining together, joining forces, or uniting as

are solicited: are asked for, requested, applied for, or sought

Call centre agents act as "secretary"

Negative examples *have had harmful effects on* the image of call centres. But the successful *collaboration* between a call centre and an industrial company shows that it can work with a different *approach*.

If sales representatives schedule all of their appointments themselves, they come under time pressure. That is why Heinz Maisel, CEO for Stäubli Tec-Systems Connectors from Bayreuth, decided to collaborate with the CommuniCall Contact Center, also located in Bayreuth.

*"Each call centre agent who works for Stäubli only **sets up appointments** for the sales representatives **assigned to him**,"* explains Alexander Bernreiter, who *is in charge of* the Austrian sales territory. *"You could call us the sales force's secretary."* Bernreiter and his colleagues make it a point not *to convey* to the customer that an anonymous call centre is calling but a colleague from the sales force. If the customer has questions or wants *to postpone* an appointment, he contacts the agent, who, upon request, gets him in contact with the sales representative or arranges for the customer to be called back immediately.

In order *to avoid* a *clashing* of appointments, the call centre agents schedule customer visits two weeks ahead of time. The agents *enter* the dates into Teamspace's Internet-based appointment calendar, *which can be accessed* at any time by the sales representatives and where they enter their own appointment dates, scheduled with their key accounts.

The sales representatives also inform their "secretary" which routes they are driving. *"We're using postal zones and schedule appointments only with those customers who are located within the **allotted** zone,"* explains Marco Dünkel.

Close dialogue with the sales force

It is the call centre agents' **uppermost** goal to schedule qualified appointments for the sales force, *"Once a week we receive feedback from the sales representatives on **what became of** our appointments,"* says Marco Dünkel. Because of the close dialogue with the Stäubli sales force or with the regional sales managers, the call centre agents are able to optimise their actions continually. This involves, for example, analysing the requirement and determining the right contact. *"In 90% of all cases, it is the production manager,"* reports Marco Dünkel. Still, he has to ask precisely each time. *"In some companies, there are several contacts and sometimes I have to contact them individually."*

If an appointment is set up, it is always confirmed to the customer in writing; however, not before the next day, as Alexander Bernreiter emphasises. *"It could happen that the sales representatives also scheduled new appointments but didn't enter them into the appointment calendar until the evening. Therefore, we*

Well prepared

Before the call centre employees were able to start scheduling the sales representatives' appointments, they received **thorough** training from customer Stäubli. Because the company sells products **which are in need of explanation**, such as a **variety of couplings**, robots for industrial needs, and a wide range of industrial **accessories**, the call centre agents **had to acquaint themselves intensely with** the new **matter**. In addition, the call centre agents receive **continuous** training at Stäubli, usually **conducted by** one of the regional sales managers. "Of course, we don't need the complete technical know-how but at least enough of it to determine the customer's requirement," says call centre agent Marco Dünkel.

If the customer asks **more probing** questions over the phone, the moment has come to schedule an appointment. "Then you reply to the customer that it's best if a sales representative explains the details," says Alexander Bernreiter.

compare the dates before we confirm the visit to the customer by e-mail or fax."

Conclusion: Because of excellent coordination and a continuous dialogue, the collaboration between the call centre agents and the sales force is being steadily optimised.

Palabras para recordar

to have harmful effects on something: to have damaging results or consequences for something

collaboration: partnership, alliance, association

approach: method, technique, style, manner, modus operandi

to set up appointments: to arrange, plan, or organise visits with customers

to be assigned to someone: to be allocated, allotted, apportioned, or commissioned to someone

to be in charge of: to be in command or control of

to convey: to communicate, to get across, to make known, to impart

to postpone: to put off, to delay, to rearrange, to reschedule, to defer

to avoid: to steer clear of, to keep away from, to shun

clashing: conflict, coincidence, concurrence

to enter: to mark down, to record, to register, to put down

which can be accessed: which can be opened, retrieved, logged on to, or read

allotted: designated, chosen, selected, assigned

uppermost: primary, main, principal, greatest, most important

what became of something: what happened to or what was the outcome of something

(continúa)

Continuación

thorough: in-depth, exhaustive, systematic, comprehensive, intensive

which are in need of explanation: which must be given details on, made clear, clarified, or elucidated

a variety of couplings: an assortment or a selection of mechanical devices that join or connect two parts

accessories: attachments, extras, add-ons, parts

to have to acquaint oneself intensely with: to have to familiarise oneself thoroughly with

matter: subject, topic, issue

continuous: non-stop, incessant,

constant, permanent conducted by: carried out, performed, run, organised, or handled by

more probing: more detailed, in-depth, or penetrating

Customer service boosts sales

Your colleagues from customer service may be able to provide you with hot sales *leads*. Therefore, it *pays off* to keep in contact with them.

The customer service reps from a medium-sized factory in Krefeld have long since gotten used to the following ritual: If the doorbell rings at their branch office at 11 A.M. on Fridays, it is Manfred G., the colleague from the field sales force. He comes in, shakes hands with everyone and exchanges a few words about the weather, the upcoming vacation, or the local soccer team's weekend match.

An *outside observer*, watching this scene, may arrive at the opinion that Manfred G. is not necessarily one of the most **industrious** people in his **guild**. He **seemingly dawdles** with his colleagues instead of taking care of his customers.

High benefit

But one couldn't be more wrong. The hour he spends at the customer service branch provides Manfred G. with high benefit. During the small talk, he hears things he never would have found out otherwise. For example, a customer service rep **recently** told him that the machine, installed at a customer's in Ettlingen, is showing **considerable signs of wear**. To Manfred G., this information was **ready cash**: "*I called there immediately and got an appointment, which gives me the opportunity to introduce our new product to the customer*". Manfred G. is certain that he will return from this appointment with an order.

Valuable lead

A lead, coming from the staff members of a customer from Hamburg and **overheard** by one of Manfred G.'s customer service colleagues, proved to be a "real **stroke of luck**" for the technical sales representative. "*Company… plans on moving to Poland!*". The following week, Manfred G. already had a meeting with the company's general manager and made him an offer: "*In case you're planning to open a production **site** in Poland, may we…?*" Manfred G. still remembers the customer's reply: "*I think you **got a hotline to Heaven!**"

However, the service technicians do not always pass on something positive to him: "*They also tell me when a customer complains about quality defects or when they discover a competitor's machine. My colleagues know that I will always listen to this sort of information.*" What's more: "*When they're at the customer's **premises**, they do far more than take care of their regular work. They talk to the operating staff and to the **foreman**. If they happen to meet the **head of engineering**, they always exchange a few words* *with him. My colleagues are always **on the lookout for** valuable tips and leads."*

Extended *arm*

To Manfred G., the customer service department has long since become the extended arm of the sales department. Much has become routine. Since the beginning of the year, every evening the service branch secretary faxes him the service technicians' work reports. *"Now I'm able **to keep track of** which machines are standing at what customer's, how old those machines are, what condition they're in, and where it may be worthwhile to inquire about **replacement purchases**."*

From time to time the customer service reps even take on selling **tasks on behalf of** Manfred G., *"They may ask the production manager if a machine's **achievement** potential is still **sufficient** and if it wouldn't be better to use a product with a higher **processing speed**. Or they bring along prospectuses **featuring** our new products and explain to him the benefits those offer."* If the customer shows even a **trace** of interest, Manfred G. gets informed about it right away.

It is not just **due to** the service reps' collegiality that the information **source** "customer service" flows so well. It's has a great deal to do with Manfred G. He does **not leave it at** saying "thank you" but sometimes invites the whole team to dinner at a restaurant.

If he managed to turn a small lead into a lucrative sale, then he is quite **generous** toward the tip provider: In the case of the company expanding business to Poland, Manfred G.'s "thank you" to his service colleagues **consisted of** a digital camera.

Palabras para recordar

to boost: to increase, to expand, to raise, to add to, to improve, to amplify

lead: hint, suggestion, recommendation, information, pointer

to pay off: to meet with success, to get results, to be effective or profitable

outside observer: uninvolved watcher, onlooker, eyewitness, or bystander

industrious: hardworking, productive, busy, conscientious, diligent, active

guild: line of work, profession, line of business

seemingly: apparently, on the face of it, ostensibly

to dawdle: to waste or kill time, to idle, to linger, to dilly-dally

recently: not long ago, just, a short time ago

considerable: substantial, extensive, great, noticeable, significant

sign of wear: symptom or evidence of deterioration

ready cash: money in the pocket

overheard: listened in on, eavesdropped on

stroke of luck: fortunate or opportune coincidence

site: plant, factory

to have a hotline to Heaven: to be intuitive, psychic, telepathic, or second sighted

to discover: to come across, to find, to detect, to encounter, to locate

premises: grounds, building, location, property, place

foreman: overseer, supervisor, chief

(continúa)

Continuación

head of engineering: person in charge or in command of manufacturing

to be on the lookout for: to be in search for or pursuit of

extended: stretched out, outstretched, spread out

to keep track of something: to keep up with, to follow, to monitor

replacement purchases: substitute or alternative acquisitions

task: job, duty, chore, assignment

on behalf of: for, representing, as a representative of, in the interests of

achievement: performance, operation, running, working

sufficient: good enough, adequate

processing speed: operational pace

to feature: to present, to introduce, to highlight, to promote, to emphasise

trace: bit, touch, hint, drop

due to: because of, attributable to

source: resource, well, supply, fund

to not leave it at: to not end it or stop at

generous: giving, open-handed

to consist of: to be made up of, to include, to involve, to entail

Make the customer a member of the team

The closer a sales representative *ties his customers* to his company and involves them in important processes, the more profitable it can be for both sides.

> *Skilled* sales representatives are not just familiar with their customers' world. They also make sure that a customer identifies himself with the supplier's world. Therefore, turning their customers into team members is an important factor of success to these sales representatives. In this way they *secure* their customers' loyalty.

Successful companies demonstrate what such teamwork can look like by involving their customers in the innovation and product development process. Here, the sales force is the most important *link* and *mediator* between customer and company. The sales force establishes the necessary contacts and *sees to it* that the customers' wishes are *passed on* promptly to the company.

Permanent exchange of ideas

An especially intensive kind of teamwork with customers takes place at a *mechanical engineering company* in Baden-Württemberg. Their development manager also *acts as* sales engineer. Together with his customers, he analyses their manufacturing processes and determines where there is *room for improvement*. In close contact with public and private *research establishments* as well as suppliers, new technologies and procedures are developed further within the company resulting in a practical solution for the customer.

The great advantage here is that the customers *contribute* to their own *tailor-made* solutions

Choosing suitable customers

Not every customer *is suited alike* for becoming a team member in the supplier's company. Above all, try to win over those who:

✔ Are especially representative for your main or desired target group. It is *crucial* that their wishes, *expectations*, and impulses are important to many other customers.

✔ Are especially suited as referral customers and as advertisement for you and your company. These are, *primarily*, representatives of well-known companies but can also be *esteemed*, influential, and *opinion-forming public figures*.

✔ Speak their mind openly and honestly and make constructive suggestions for improvement. You will have to use your experience and *assessment to figure out* who *ranks among* these loyal customers. Often, customers who are not yet satisfied with your offer turn out to be good providers of ideas and *leads*.

✔ Are *doers* and not just develop ideas but also *implement* them *single-mindedly* in their company.

in their supplier's company. The sales engineer uses the on-going exchange of ideas with his customers to determine *current* and future product requirements. The customers, again, are involved so closely in the product development process that they cannot help but stay loyal to their supplier.

Palabras para recordar

to tie someone to something: to bind or commit someone to something

skilled: able, good, accomplished, competent, capable, experienced, proficient

to secure: to acquire, to obtain, to get, to come by, to get hold of

link: connection, relation, tie, bond

(continúa)

Continuación

mediator: go-between, intermediary, facilitator, middleman

to see to it: to take care, to arrange, to organise, to be responsible

to pass on: to forward, to transmit, to send, to dispatch

mechanical engineering company: machine or engine-building firm

to act as: to serve as, to fulfill the function of, to do the work of a

room for improvement: potential for development, possibilities for enhancement

research establishment: investigation, fact-finding, or exploration institute

to contribute to: to play a part or role in, to collaborate on, to work on

tailor-made: custom-made, specially made, made to order, made to measure

current: present, existing, recent

to be suited alike: to be appropriate, right, or qualified in the same way

crucial: decisive, critical, determining, pivotal, important, essential

expectations: outlook, speculation, prospects, hopes

primarily: above all, mainly, for the most part, mostly, in the first place

esteemed: respected, admired, valued, honoured, revered, highly thought of

opinion-forming: point of view-shaping or determining

public figure: celebrity, celebrated public character, very important person

assessment: estimation, judgement, evaluation, appraisal

(continúa)

Continuación

to figure out: to understand, to comprehend, to make out, to see, to reason

to rank among: to belong to the group of, to fit within the circle of

lead: tip, hint, pointer, information, clue, suggestion

doer: go-getter, achiever, organiser, active person

to implement: to put into practice, to apply, to realise, to put into effect

single-mindedly: determinedly, persistently, resolutely, tenaciously, steadfastly

The sales representative as market researcher?

The sales representative is often called the company's *foremost* market researcher. Certainly he can ask "market research"-type questions during the sales talk, but there are a number of things *that need to be taken into account*, because there may be some risk involved.

Palabras para recordar

foremost: leading, principal, top, primary, most important, chief, prime

that need to be taken into account: that must be taken into consideration or kept in mind

prospects: potential, possibilities, promise, expectations

current: present, existing, recent, present-day

pertaining to: relating to, concerning, being relevant to

interfering: bothersome, annoying, irritating, disruptive

Example layout for a field report for market research

Field report with regard to the market situation:

1st quarter 20XX

Sales representative   Territory   Date

1. Three important new projects:

   ✔ (Customer/project/order volume/***prospects***/competition/what needs to be done?)

2. Three important projects that were lost:

   ✔ (Customer/project/order volume/lost to/what should have been done?)

3. The ***current*** most important customer demands ***pertaining to:***

   ✔ Problem solving

   ✔ Product/assortment

   ✔ Service/after-sales service

   ✔ Customer information

   ✔ Pricing/conditions

   ✔ Organisation of customer service and processing

4. Our competitors' three most ***interfering*** activities right now:

   ✔ (Who/which activity/where/in what situation)

5. Suggestions for more success:

   ✔ Comments, requests, etc.

Capítulo 3

Vender en inglés

*L*a venta es el motor que hace funcionar una empresa. Pero hay que tener en cuenta que el camino hasta llegar a ella está plagado de trampas y peligros que dificultan su andadura. El primer requisito para llegar a la meta es conocer bien el camino (tener toda la posible información del potencial cliente) y estar motivado. En segundo lugar habrá que saber elegir en cada momento la vía correcta (es decir, de entre todos los recursos posibles de venta, seleccionar la técnica adecuada, aquella que nos acerque al cliente). Y, por último, habrá que saber sortear los baches del camino (resolver los conflictos con el cliente, para que quede siempre satisfecho y mantenga la confianza en nosotros).

Aunque, sin duda, el recorrido es complicado, en este capítulo te ayudaremos a convertirte en un as de las ventas. Ponte ropa cómoda, cálzate las zapatillas y ¡prepárate para el trayecto!

The salesperson makes the difference

A product's price and quality plays an important role in the customers' buying decision. However, there is more to it if you want to keep customers long-term. That is why the Winkler Group invests highly in the qualification of its sales staff.

Investing in its sales force is for Winkler, a specialist for **commercial vehicle spare parts** and accessories headquartered in Stuttgart, an important aspect **contributing to** success. Aside from in-house training courses and **advanced training**, Winkler provides special workshops on the subject "**Assertive** Selling," **conducted by** sales trainer Thorsten Hartmann from Bexbach. *"It is important to us that the workshops **are custom-tailored** to our company,"* explains managing director Rüdiger Hahn.

Longterm cooperation Winkler continuously trains the approximately 200 members of their sales staff at their individual **branches**. All year round, workshops take place **under the direction of** sales trainer Thorsten Hartmann. The participants are usually made up of 12 to 14 salespeople from a regional branch. Because Hartmann has been working long-term with Winkler, he **is very much in tune with** the company and its **particularities**. Hartmann **turns special attention to** Winkler's central service idea and **encourages** the sales staff **to internalise it** and put it into practice. The sales representatives are to offer their customers not just individual spare parts but complete packages (**"everything from one source"**). On the other hand, the customer has **to sense** that the salesperson does everything in his or her power to fulfill his wishes and takes every wish seriously.

In addition, Thorsten Hartmann occasionally **accompanies** sales representatives on their customer visits for training on the job.

It's all about the customer

"The workshops are all about the customer," says Markus Fuß, Team Leader Sales for the customer groups **repair shops** and bus companies and Martin Rüter, Team Leader Sales for the customer groups **vehicle owners** and **shipping agencies** at the Dortmund branch.

Martin Rüter gives an example: *"We really **delved into** the issue of **competitive advantage**. The point was **to determine** in what areas we **have an edge on** our competitors."* Now, Martin Rüter and his sales colleagues are able to implement the results of their **considerations** immediately: *"One such competitive advantage is the ability to deliver several times daily, while some competitors manage to deliver only once a day."*

The customer development conversation

An especially important part of the workshops deals with the subject of "customer development conversations." *"Each conversation that helps me **to move forward with** the customer is a customer development conversation,"* explains Markus Fuß. For example, it is already viewed as a customer development conversation if the sales representative gains new information about the customer even if he wasn't able **to prompt** him to buy. *"After each conversation the sales representative should examine whether it was a customer development conversation or a standstill,"* says Fuß.

The salesperson decides the issue

In the opinion of Markus Fuß and Martin Rüter, Winkler's **decisive** competitive advantage is made up of the competence and friendliness of its sales staff. They **are convinced** that, ultimately, a customer **can only be** won and **retained** by the sales-person's persona. *"If a customer is tied so closely to the company because of the salesperson, he doesn't have any **desire*** *to leave. He then shows little interest if a competitor offers some products at a lower price,"* says Markus Fuß. However, if the customer *is too focused on* "his" sales representative, that may present some danger. *"The customer should be able to trust in the other members of the sales staff and deal with them, too, if his favourite sales representative **happens to be away on holiday**."*

Conclusion: It's all about is the personal relationship with the customer. It is the basis for a long-term, successful relationship.

The Winkler Group, headquartered in Stuttgart, is represented in 14 German locations and one location each in Switzerland and Russia. Its clientele *is comprised* of commercial vehicle owners, such as shipping agencies, construction or *waste disposal* companies, bus companies, repair shops, farmers, and international trade partners.

Palabras para recordar

to make the difference: to decide the issue, to clinch matters

commercial vehicle: utility van, bus, or lorry

spare part: replacement element, substitute component

contributing to: being instrumental or having a hand in achieving

advanced training: further schooling

assertive: forceful, aggressive, dynamic

conducted by: organised or managed by

to be custom-tailored to: to be designed for, adapted to, or custom-made for

branch: local office, division, area office

under the direction of: headed, led, run, or managed by

(continúa)

Continuación

to be very much in tune with something: to be in accord, harmony, or concurrence with something

particularities: individual characteristics, features, or attributes

to turn special attention to: to direct particular awareness toward

to encourage: to persuade, to convince, to influence

to internalise something: to assimilate something, to take something in

everything from one source: all from the same supplier or originator

to sense: to get the impression, to have a feeling, to perceive

to accompany: to go with, to escort

repair shop: workshop, auto body shop

vehicle owner: registered or recorded keeper

shipping agency: forwarding or hauling company

to delve into: to explore, to enquire into, to examine, to research

competitive advantage: having an edge over the rival or opponent

to determine: to clarify, to ascertain, to verify, to establish

to have an edge on someone: to have an advantage or the lead on someone

consideration: thought, deliberation, contemplation, reflection

to move forward with someone: to make headway, make progress, or gain ground with someone

to prompt: to induce, to persuade, to encourage, to tempt

(continúa)

Continuación

decisive: deciding, determining, critical, crucial, most important

to be convinced: to be sure, certain, positive, or confident

can only be retained: can just be kept, preserved, held on to, or maintained

desire: need, aspiration, inclination

to be too focused on someone: to be too attached to or emotionally involved with someone

to happen to be away on holiday: to turn out to be on vacation

to be comprised of: to include, to consist of, to encompass

waste disposal: removal of refuse

Liven up *your* e-mails *and* letters

Following are suggestions to make your messages more effective:

✔ Start with a *persuasive* one-liner. Whether posed as a question or statement, this should be interesting and benefit-oriented. For example: "You can save up to 40 % on your printing costs."

✔ *Assume* a conversational tone. Avoid *sophisticated* language and sound natural.

✔ Make reading quick and easy. Keep it *brief* and simple by avoiding *long drawn-out* sentences and limiting *paragraph* length to six lines.

✔ *Emphasise* benefits. Make your letters customer-centred and keep repeating the advantages.

✔ Direct the customer repeatedly. *Trigger* action by telling the customer what to do several times. For example, if you want him to call your toll-free number, work the number into your letter multiple times.

Palabras para recordar

to liven up: to put some life into, to put some spark into, to add some zest to, to give a boost to

persuasive: compelling, convincing, gripping, effective

to assume: to take up, to take on, to adopt, to come to have

sophisticated: complicated, complex

brief: short, to the point, concise, succinct, compact

long drawn-out: stretched out, dragged out, protracted, lengthy

paragraph: section, subdivision, segment

to emphasise: to highlight, to stress, to call attention to, to underline, to give prominence to

to trigger: to cause, to generate, to bring about, to prompt

Supervise *yourself properly*

In the *fast-paced*, everyday life of selling, these few timeless principles will help you to keep your self-management in check:

✔ Orientation towards results. The *touchstone* is the achievement of set goals and the completion of tasks.

✔ Make a contribution to the whole. Aside from the expectations that come with the position, always *set your sights on* the *superior objectives* of the company as well.

✔ Concentrate on the basics. *Pool* available strengths and concentrate them on carefully chosen objectives.

✔ Use already existing *forces*. Focus on *what is at your disposal* and not just on the correction of *deficiencies*.

✔ Gain trust. This *mainly affects* the quality of the office climate and the corporate culture, as well as the contact with customers.

✔ Think positive. Display a stronger orientation towards opportunities, instead of pointing out problems.

These principles regulate and *lastingly secure* the quality of everyday tasks and *facilitate* the implementation of the right *set of tools* necessary to fulfill them. They *comprise* the *core* of what can also be understood as corporate culture.

Palabras para recordar

to supervise: to manage, to direct, to control, to take charge of

fast-paced: hurried, hasty, fleet-footed, accelerated, brisk

touchstone: criterion, yardstick, benchmark, acid test, standard

to set one's sights on: to aim at, to aspire to, to strive toward, to work toward

superior objectives: higher goals, ambitions, intentions, targets, or ideas

to pool: to combine, to bundle, to merge, to group

forces: strengths, powers, strong points, assets, plus points

what is at your disposal: what you already have available or on hand

deficiency: weakness, imperfection, insufficiency, flaw, shortcoming, weak point

(continúa)

Continuación

to mainly affect: to mostly have an effect on, influence, or have an impact on

to lastingly secure: to continually ensure, assure, guarantee, or underwrite

to facilitate: to smooth the path of, to make possible, to make easier, to make smoother

set of tools: instruments

to comprise: to make up, to form, to constitute, to compose

core: centre, central part, heart, essence, quintessence, nitty-gritty

Raise awareness by asking the right questions

When you're analysing a customer's requirements, the important thing is to raise his awareness by asking the right questions.

Salespeople who bombard their customers with a whole catalogue of questions will quickly *encounter rejection*. It is much better, especially when *conducting* a requirement analysis, to use certain question types strategically. The four most important ones are:

1. Questions about the situation.

They serve to find out more about the customer and his *current* situation. Therefore, they need to be asked immediately after the greeting and "warm up" phase.

Typical situational questions are, for example:

✔ *Which system are you currently operating with?*

✔ *Have you ever **looked into**…?*

✔ *How many of your office workplaces are **equipped with** this kind of installation?*, etc.

However, there is great danger in asking situational questions because they may **drift into triteness**, that's to say the customer is asked questions which you should have been able to answer **beforehand**. This includes information about the business areas, industrial locations, international activities, number of employees and, of course, the company's product and service portfolio.

Therefore, try to collect such information ahead of time and **have it reconfirmed** by the customer so you can add a **related** question. Here are some examples:

✔ *You are currently planning an expansion to…
By doing so, how do you solve the following problem …?*

✔ *You are represented in five other industrial locations. How do you handle the coordination of…?*, etc.

2. Questions about problems.

These questions **probe deeper into** the actual requirement analysis. Your goal is to determine in what areas the customer is dissatisfied or has difficulties or to make him aware of it in the first place. Examples:

✔ *How difficult is the coordination of…?*

✔ *How costly is it to service these machines…?*

✔ *How often do **breakdowns** happen in…?*

It's typical for problem questions that indeed they turn a concrete, possible problem into a subject of discussion to which the customer has to say something. However, if it turns out that the problem does not exist for the customer, you will have to change your strategy. Basically, there are two possibilities: You *jump to* the next point and talk about another possible problem or you try, by asking a related question, to raise the customer's awareness and direct his attention to aspects he has not considered before.

This quick decision is often *a walk on a tightrope*. Therefore, first ask situation questions, get a clear picture of the customer's possible requirement and only then start asking problem questions.

3. Questions about consequences.

Once you were able to raise the customer's problem awareness, you need *to paint a vivid picture of* the negative consequences. Only by doing so will the customer realise that there is a *call for action*. Questions about consequences are, therefore, always future-oriented. Examples:

✔ *Won't these technical problems become even bigger if you open and **interlink** additional branch offices?*

✔ *Isn't there a **high risk of failure** if you're operating with technology that keeps breaking down?*

It is important not to recommend a solution in this phase but to increase the customer's *psychological strain*. The more drastically you present the possible *implications* by asking questions about consequences, the more he *yearns for* a solution.

4. Questions about solutions.

Now the time is right to guide the customer's attention from the problem to the solution. Ask him how he *envisions* an ideal solution. Examples:

✔ *In your opinion, what needs to be done to keep this risk at a minimum?*

✔ *What would you wish for that would **rid you** of this **worry** in the future?*

✔ *In your opinion, what standard does such a system have to meet?*

Your questions ***are supposed to*** encourage the customer to actively formulate desired solutions. Listen ***attentively*** and take notes. Then you will be prepared when you demonstrate to the customer how your solution is the way he imagines it to be.

Palabras para recordar

to raise awareness: to increase

to encounter rejection: to be faced with a negative response, a refusal, or a snub

to conduct: to do, to carry out, to perform, to handle

current: present, existing, present-day

to look into: to explore, to investigate, to research, to make inquires about

to be equipped with: to be fitted out, provided, furnished, or supplied with

to drift into triteness: to become banal, commonplace, hackneyed, trivial, or prosaic

beforehand: earlier, in advance, ahead of time, before now

to have something reconfirmed: to have something once again verified, substantiated, or validated

related: connected, associated, accompanying, linked, correlated

to probe deeper into something: to get closer to the core of something

breakdown: interruption, stopping, stoppage, failure, malfunctioning

(continúa)

Continuación

to jump to: to immediately address, concentrate on, or take up

a walk on a tightrope: a high-wire act, a razor-edge affair

to paint a vivid picture of something: to make something crystal-clear

call for action: need or requirement to do something

to interlink: to interconnect, to cross-link

high risk of failure: strong chance for breakdown, stoppage, or non-function

psychological strain: mental stress, emotional suffering

implications: repercussions, effects, impact, outcome

to yearn for something: to desire, long for, crave, or hunger for something

to envision: to imagine, to envisage, to picture, to see in one's mind's eye, to foresee

to rid someone of something: to free, liberate, unburden, or relieve someone of something

worry: concern, anxiety, trouble, apprehension, care

are supposed to: are meant, intended, or expected to

attentively: carefully, alertly, conscientiously

Emotionalising the sales approach

In their sales approach, Fleurop AG is *relying on* highly different *measures*: from the business to customer approach, with its classic advertising spots, to cross marketing and business to business campaigns.

Especially in the business customer area, flowers are an effective means for *triggering* emotions and for *pleasantly surprising* customers. More and more account managers use the flower approach with their prospective customers: A study on the use of advertising media in customer relationship management, *conducted by* the market research institute Skopos, *gives proof* that more than 40% of marketing executives think of flowers as an effective means to win over new customers.

Fleurop's growing number of business customers are *attended to* by a special division named FleuropCadeaux. In the beginning of May 2005, this business to business service launched an unusual campaign: The floristic provider *called on* all companies nationwide to *enrol* for the "FleuropCadeaux Business Day 2005" to be held on September 13. *"This day provided an opportunity for all participating companies to approach potential customers on an emotional level and to make new contacts,"* explains a Fleurop manager. What's special: the *bouquets* could be created in the style of the customer's corporate design. In order *to persuade* as many companies as possible to send floral greetings to new customers, a registered customer, on this day, had to pay only five euros, including a service charge, instead of the official price of 27 euros for an individually arranged company bouquet.

Another factor *contributing to* Fleurop's success is the company's online *involvement*. For years, Fleurop's partners have been profiting from the possibility of online order placing, which is especially popular among business customers. According to the computer and technical analysis of the Institut für Demoskopie Allensbach, the user-friendly online shop www.fleurop.de counts among the most frequented German Internet retail stores. To prove this: While the total number of online buyers increased by about ten percent in comparison to the previous year, according

to the Allensbach study the number of Fleurop
Internet customers increased by one third. For next
year, the company is expecting another ***two-digit***
increase in online sales.

Aside from precisely coordinating all advertising
measures, such as e-mail marketing, banner
ads, and POS ***tools*** for the classic advertising
activities, partnering with ***candy manufacturer***
Ferrero (brands, among others, are Mon Chéri,
Rocher) proved to be very successful. Flower
coupons, ***attached to*** special campaign packages,
allow customers to get discounts at the Fleurop
shops.

Matching its products' emotional orientation,
Fleurop AG plans to increase its involvement in the
area of corporate citizenship. During June, July, and
August of last year, Fleurop offered so-called "UNICEF
bouquets." From the sale of each bouquet, four
euros were ***donated to*** the United Nations Children's
Fund. The customer donated two euros and Fleurop
added the other two. A highly effective measure for
customer management.

Various studies give proof that a company's
extensive social engagement, such as Fleurop's,
shows an immediate increase in sales, ***not to mention***
the effect of positive ***brand perception*** by the
customers.

Conclusion: By employing varied measures,
Fleurop AG manages to display a positive
presence in a variety of target groups
from the end user to business to business
customers. The business to business area
is developing into a highly successful
enterprise where Fleurop is keeping ***custom-
tailored***, individual offers ***available***.

Palabras para recordar

sales approach: selling method, tactic, or style

to rely on: to bank on, to trust in, to count on, to bet on

measures: ways, methods, channels, courses, instruments

to trigger: to activate, to set off, to generate, to prompt, to elicit

to pleasantly surprise someone: to delightfully astonish or astound someone

conducted by: carried out by, done by, performed by

to give proof: to produce evidence, verification, or confirmation

to be attended to: to be taken care of, dealt with, or given one's attention to

to call on: to appeal to, to ask, to request, to urge

to enrol: to register, to sign up, to put one's name down

bouquet: bunch or spray of flowers

to persuade someone to do something: to convince, sway, or induce someone to do something

to contribute to: to be conducive to, to lead to, to be instrumental in

involvement: engagement, commitment

two-digit: any number between 10 and 99

aside from: apart from, notwithstanding

tools: instruments, means

candy manufacturer: sweets producer, confectionary maker

attached to: fixed to, fastened to, stuck to, affixed to

matching: to go with, to complement, to harmonise with

donated to: given to, contributed to, bestowed upon, provided for

(continúa)

Continuación
various: numerous, many, a number of
not to mention: not counting, not including, to say nothing of, in addition to
brand perception: trademark recognition, awareness, or cognizance
custom-tailored: customised, made to order, custom-made
to keep something available: to keep something on hand, obtainable, or ready

Correct assessment of *customer inquiries*

All the efforts the sales department puts into the acquisition of a new customer often turn out *to be in vain* because the prospect decides to buy from the competitor after all. One *corrective measure to prevent this* is a *substantiated* calculation of the buying *probability* for each customer inquiry.

In principle, it is true that each customer inquiry has to be answered as quickly, competently, and *comprehensively* as possible. But businesses have *to bear cost-effectiveness in mind* and can't allow themselves *to pay the same degree of attention to each prospect*.

The internationally operating market research firm Vocatus, based in Munich, developed a model called lead scoring, which supports companies in the assessment of customer inquires. Based on statistical procedures, each inquiry receives a purchasing probability score.

The problem is that *"a large number of inquires score very low in buying probability,"* says Mark Lendrich, Senior Project Manager for Vocatus, and illustrates this fact by using the example of an automobile manufacturer examined by Vocatus. In this case, 23 % of the customers produce 81 % of sales. Lead scoring provides an extremely precise *prediction* model. A process called data mining identifies influential factors that show a high *connection with* purchasing probability. Factors, such as customer type, socio-demographic data (such as age or *gender*) and all other *available* data about the customer *are taken into account*. During the examination, the market researchers try to analyse the customers on the basis of data *collected* from order forms that the prospects completed online on the car maker's website.

Aside from the fact that some customers do not fully complete the form, aspects such as the age of their current car or the amount of *extras are incorporated* in the evaluation. *"In some companies we experienced that prospects **going to great trouble over** filling in the form, score higher in purchasing probability,"* explains Lendrich. But even *less obvious* connections to buying probability can be discovered this way: A prospect who completes the website form and also uses two or more different modules on the website and configures many typical extras into the vehicle scores, statistically, a buying probability of 97 %. Another prospect, being only 20 years of age but otherwise showing the same data only scores a buying probability of 5 %.

But *"a prospect **is not more inclined** to buy a car because of his **repeated** contacts with the manufacturer,"* **underlines** Lendrich, *"**rather it can be determined** statistically that those customers who had repeated contact, have a higher buying probability."* In this way, certain customer inquiries will take priority. This makes lead scoring an important tool, for example, in the sales support for dealers. *"At the same time, customer inquiries can be dealt with more efficiently, which in turn increases the company's*

profitability and sales," says market researcher
Lendrich.

Palabras para recordar

assessment: appraisal, evaluation, rating, estimation,
judgement, review

to be in vain: to be unsuccessful, ineffective, useless,
futile, or unproductive

corrective measure: remedial or counteractive course
of action

to prevent something: to stop or avoid something

substantiated: backed up, validated

probability: likelihood, possibility, odds

comprehensively: completely, thoroughly, exhaustively,
in detail, carefully

to bear cost-effectiveness in mind: to think economically,
to remember to save expenses

to pay the same degree of attention to each prospect: to
concentrate one's efforts equally on each potential client

prediction: forecast, calculation

connection with: link to, association with, relationship
with, correlation to

gender: sex, masculinity or femininity

available: obtainable, accessible, existing

to be taken into account: to be considered, to be taken into
consideration

collected: gathered, brought together, pulled together,
accumulated

aside from: besides, apart from, except for, with the
exception of

extras: optional or special equipment

(continúa)

Continuación

to be incorporated: to be included or integrated

to go to great trouble over something: to go to great pains over or make a big effort in doing something

less obvious: not so noticeable, apparent, or evident

to be not more inclined to do something: to be not more prone, of a mind, apt, or disposed to do something

repeated: recurring, repetitive, frequent

to underline: to underscore, to emphasise, to highlight

rather: more exactly, more accurately

it can be determined: it can be verified, ascertained, or established

---

Successfully dealing with buying conflicts

Most customers go through some inner conflicts before they finally make the decision to buy. *Recognise* those conflicts and *guide your customers through them*.

It takes a certain amount of *psychological strain* before customers are ready to deal with a product. *"The customer has to recognise that he has a problem and long for a solution,"* explains a sales representative from the plastics industry.

Sales trainers speak in this context of buying conflicts. Hans A. Hey, a sales trainer from Heilbronn, explains that a customer experiences several types of conflict until the final closing. *"These conflicts cause him tension."* As a rule, customers experience three or sometimes four types of conflict:

✔ The requirement conflict.

✔ The offer conflict.

✔ The closing conflict.

✔ The responsibility conflict.

The requirement conflict

The requirement conflict is the *prerequisite* for the customer to consider in the first place whether he needs a product or a solution. The essential question, therefore, is: *"Do I need the product/ the solution or not?"* According to Hey, you're also talking about a requirement conflict if the customer is dissatisfied with his *present* supplier or has problems with the product he's currently using. In this case, the customer *perceives* his situation as being *unsatisfactory* but doesn't know yet how to resolve it.

Such a situation is ideal for Mark S., a sales representative for an IT service provider, *"A potential customer's dissatisfaction is the best prerequisite for him to be ready to make a change. The psychological strain just has to be big enough."* In this situation, Mark S. likes to steer things in the right direction, *"I can explain to the customer what will happen if he keeps operating with **outdated** systems. Then it's all the more effective when I show him possibilities for bringing his technology back to being **state-of-the-art**, which will allow him to work much more efficiently and **largely** without risk."*

The offer conflict

Mark S. knows, of course, that not every customer buys immediately. *"You always have to **assume** that the customer **obtains** offers from competitors."* In Hans A. Hey's opinion, this *constitutes* a typical offer conflict. The customer is asking himself whether the sales representative's offer really represents the optimal solution or if there are other, better suppliers out there. *"Basically, a customer, who has decided to* *obtain a new solution, finds himself in the offer conflict phase,"* says Hey.

For this situation, the trainer gives the following advice: The sales representative should explain to the customer why his offer meets his requirements especially well or *exceeds* the competitor's offer and how it *is tailored to* his individual needs. The more precisely the sales representative has determined the customer's requirement, the more concretely he can use it in his sales argumentation.

The closing conflict

The critical phase towards the end of the sales process can ruin all the work you put into it beforehand.

According to the experience of Hans A. Hey, a customer may *suffer* a closing conflict even if he *was convinced of* the sales representative's solution before. In order to get the customer through the closing, the sales representative has to give him a good reason why he should buy now. As a rule, concrete facts, such as a lower-priced *introductory* offer or the *urgency* of the decision because the customer may suffer negative consequences if he keeps working with outdated technology, *are suitable* for this situation.

The responsibility conflict

Some decision makers are afraid of making a mistake and *being called to account for it*. Or they have to *vindicate themselves* to their company for the high costs. This may *trigger* great fear.

The higher the investment, the more likely a responsibility conflict *emerges*. In this situation, Hey recommends taking the customers' concerns very seriously or even address them in advance and explain how risks can be kept at a minimum.

Conclusion: Basically, buying conflicts are positive because they generate psychological strain and the pressure to do something about it. Sales representatives have to take these conflicts very seriously and support their customers mentally and emotionally as well.

Palabras para recordar

to recognise: to identify, to make out, to spot, to distinguish

to guide someone through something: to direct, to steer, or to lead someone through something

psychological strain: nervous tension, stress, anxiety, mental pressure

to long for something: to yearn for, to crave, to desire, or to wish for something

tension: worry, nervousness, apprehension, agitation

prerequisite: precondition, requisite, necessity, essential, qualification

present: current, existing, present-day, contemporary

to perceive: to sense, to feel, to understand, to realise, to recognise

unsatisfactory: unacceptable, substandard, not up to scratch, poor

outdated: obsolete, out of date, antiquated, superseded, old-fashioned

state-of-the-art: high-tech, up to date, modern

largely: mainly, mostly, essentially, by and large, for the most part, basically

to assume: to take for granted, to presume, to suppose, to presuppose

to obtain: to get, to attain, to acquire, to pick up, to get hold of

(continúa)

Continuación

to constitute: to amount to, to represent, to signify, to be regarded as, to be equivalent to

to exceed: to go beyond, to surpass, to beat, to top, to outdo

to be tailored to: to be modified, customised, adapted, or adjusted to

to suffer: to experience, to undergo, to go through, to endure

to be convinced of something: to be positive, sure, or confident about something

introductory: initial, starting, preliminary

urgency: importance, necessity, top priority, exigency, imperativeness

to be suitable: to be appropriate, fitting, apt, or right

to be called to account for something: to be requested to give reasons or show grounds for something

to vindicate oneself: to justify or defend oneself

to trigger: to cause, to generate, to prompt, to elicit, to bring about

to emerge: to materialise, to appear, to surface, to transpire, to occur

Prospecting on difficult terrain

Renate Schwittay from Berlin does not sell *tangible* products to her customers but a sense of well-being.

Renate Schwittay has *chosen* an especially difficult sales industry. She neither sells tangible products nor are there any *consolidated scientific findings* in existence about her subject area. She calls her *occupation "Health advisory service on*

environmentally compatible building materials,"
relating to "*technically and naturally induced*
***hazardous** radiation, meaning earth rays and*
*electromagnetic **pollution**.*"

"*The most important **prerequisite** for my job is to be*
*convinced of the **issue**,*" explains Renate Schwittay.
The certainty that radiation affects peoples' well-
being motivated her to change jobs. Previously, she
was employed for many years as graduate engineer
in the building industry. Because she had always
been fascinated by everything that had to do with her
current topic, she switched jobs and became a sales
partner of the franchise system "The Healthy House
– institute for health advisory on environmentally
compatible building materials" in Münster.

Lectures *serve as prospecting opportunities*

To Renate Schwittay, the basis of her selling success
lies in ***making the subject accessible to*** her
customers. To do so, she holds evening lectures in
her area, "*I start out by choosing a target group which
I think would **be the most promising**. Then I look for
an organiser who will put me in contact with this target
group.*" Such cooperation partners could be nature
conservation associations and clubs of women *from
rural areas*, senior clubs and culture circles, *adult
education centres* and the local branches of political
parties. If she can't find an appropriate *host*, Renate
Schwittay organises the lectures herself.

Attracting attention

It is especially important to Renate Schwittay to call
attention to her lectures by involving the local media.
Therefore, she goes to see the local papers' *editorial
departments* and the radio stations in order *to
prompt* them to point out the event. If this kind of
public relations work isn't successful, she *places
ads* and distributes fliers.

However, the saleslady isn't all that intent on filling the hall to the last seat. Twenty listeners are enough and she's satisfied if 10 show up, *"It's easier with a smaller group **to get the subject across**."* Renate Schwittay has to be prepared at all times that her theory about earth radiation and electromagnetic pollution may ***provoke protests*** from listeners. In this situation, she only expresses what she can take responsibility for, *"Namely, that there are no clear scientific findings if such earth radiation is **harmful** or not, but obviously there are individuals who react to it with **physical discomfort**."* Instead of getting involved in a debate, she ***prefers*** to read letters from customers. *"People actually write to me how the measures I recommended **did the trick**."*

About 20 % recommendations

The most important prospecting phase starts after the lecture has ended. Then, the participants talk about their own experiences and ask for individual advice. This is usually the point in time when appointments are scheduled. As a rule, Renate Schwittay keeps a list of all participants, and along with their addresses and phone numbers, she notes which questions the respective person asked and which health problems he or she ***addressed***. Within the next three days, she calls the participant in order to schedule an appointment at his or her home.

Such a customer visit may take up to two hours. Renate Schwittay ***measures*** the rooms and advises the residents on a suitable course of action. ***On average***, the consultant gets about five orders per lecture at a volume of about 1000 euros. Even if an order ***didn't materialise***, each customer contact has been worthwhile: *"About 20 % of my orders result from the referrals of my lecture participants."*

Palabras para recordar

to prospect: to look or search for new customers

on difficult terrain: under demanding circumstances, under tough conditions

tangible: touchable, palpable, tactile, visible

to choose: to decide on, to opt for, to go for, to select, to pick out

consolidated scientific findings: confirmed results relating to the principles of science

occupation: activity, work, profession, job, field, trade

health advisory service on environ-mentally compatible building materials: consultative facility on ecologically sound or non-polluting construction resources

relating to: applying to, having relevance to, concerning, pertaining to

hazardous: unsafe, perilous, harmful

pollution: contamination, smog, effluence, adulteration

prerequisite: requirement, qualification, necessity, precondition

issue: subject, matter, question, topic

lecture: talk, address, speech, discourse, lesson

to make something accessible to someone: to make something understandable or comprehensible to someone

to be the most promising: to be the most favourable, to show the greatest potential

from rural areas: from the countryside, from agricultural regions

adult education centre: school or educational institution for grown-ups

host: organiser, one who furnishes facilities for a function or event

(continúa)

Continuación

to attract attention: to create awareness, to draw interest or regard

editorial department: section of a publishing house where newspaper content is written up

to prompt someone to do something: to cause, induce, or encourage someone to do something

to place ads: to put notices or announcements in the newspaper

to get the subject across: to make one understand or become familiar with the topic

to provoke protest: to cause, bring about, trigger, or give rise to objection

harmful: unsafe, damaging, injurious, risky, dangerous, toxic, destructive

physical discomfort: bodily ache, pain, soreness, tenderness, or irritation

to prefer: to favour, to like better, to choose, to select

did the trick: were effective, took effect, were successful, useful, or helpful

addressed: spoke of, talked about, described, communicated

to measure: to determine the length, width, and height of

on average: normally, typically, usually

to not materialise: to not come into being, happen, occur, or come about

How to "sell" bad news well

Every now and then, sales representatives have to deliver bad news to their customers. In this situation, the right strategy is *key*.

Hardly any sales representative likes to deliver bad news to his customer, for example, an increase in price or the inability to keep a delivery date. However, especially when dealing with bad news, it is most important to communicate them in such a fashion that the customer relationship will *not suffer from it*. It is vital to avoid the following *lapses* under any circumstances:

Mistake 1

Tardily delivering the news to the customer, although it had been known for some time. By doing so, one often causes additional problems for the customer.

As soon as the circumstances of the case are clear, arrange for a meeting with the customer to notify him about the *surfacing* problems.

Mistake 2

To unnecessarily *elongate* the small talk portion of your meeting or *to beat about the bush*. The customer will become anxious and his time *gratuitously wasted*.

Get to the actual subject of conversation right after the initial greeting phase.

Mistake 3

To bad-mouth the "guilty party" in front of the customer. This will give the impression to the customer that the salesperson is *cowardly blaming* others and is indeed trying *to cover up* his own *wrongdoing*.

Accept responsibility in front of the customer and take a stand for your company.

Mistake 4

Delivering the news only by means of a formal explanatory statement. This can *come across as* quite brusque and impersonal.

Always deliver bad news personally. This will give you the opportunity to instantaneously have an influence on the customer's reaction.

Always *take into consideration*: Communicate clearly. Do not try *to conceal* or *diminish* the facts; this can create misunderstandings that the customer may blame you for afterwards, *claiming* he was not informed correctly.

Nevertheless, link the bad news to something positive: When dealing with a mishap in your company, explain to the customer what you will do now, so it will never happen again. And, naturally, you will have *to offer compensation* to your customer.

Palabras para recordar

key: important, crucial, vital

hardly any: barely any, scarcely any, almost no

not suffer from it: not be affected, afflicted, or troubled by it

lapse: slip, error, mistake, blunder

tardily: unpunctually, belatedly, slowly

surfacing: emerging, appearing, materialising, developing

to elongate: to make longer, to draw out, to extend, to stretch out

to beat about the bush: to play for time, to use delaying tactics, to drag one's feet

(continúa)

Continuación

gratuitously: needlessly, pointlessly, senselessly

wasted: used up, squandered, dissipated

to bad-mouth someone: to put someone down, to backbite or trash someone

the guilty party: the blameworthy or culpable persons

cowardly: gutlessly, spinelessly, weakly, lily-liveredly

to blame: to point the finger at, to accuse, to assign fault to, to condemn

to cover up: to conceal, to hide, to keep secret, to hush up, to keep dark

wrongdoing: professional misconduct, mistake, unprofessional behaviour

to come across as: to be perceived or understood as

to take into consideration: to bear in mind, to take into account, to be mindful or heedful of

to conceal: to hide, to keep the lid on, to screen, to cover up

to diminish: to take the edge off, to detract from, to belittle

to claim: to maintain, to argue, to assert, to declare, to profess, to allege

to offer compensation: to make amends, to put forward reparation or recompense

How to react if customers are pressed for time

It's not necessarily a *disadvantage* if the customer is under a lot of pressure time wise. The point is *to judge* the situation correctly and *seize* the opportunity.

"If the customer doesn't have time, it is easiest to sell him something." Today, many door to door salespeople still **act according to** this motto. The customer is not prepared for his visitor. He **is in a hurry** and becomes nervous. Because he doesn't have the time to think things over, he is in a weaker position. So he **is easily cajoled**, but may **be annoyed** about it later.

Competent sales representatives **are aware of the fact** that they may have **to pay dearly for throwing a customer off** like that because he may cancel the order and will be lost forever. But they still know that a customer's time pressure may be an opportunity. *"Because time is running short, most customers want to get to the point as quickly as possible. They **don't beat about the bush** and they **express** clearly and **distinctly** what they want and how they **envision** a solution. They tell you immediately if they have any doubts and they don't **make any flimsy excuses**. That is a great advantage because the cards are on the table immediately,"* explains Joseph K., a sales representative for an **outside supplier** in Bavaria.

Still tell them what it's about

To hear from a customer directly that he doesn't have any time right now happens only when Joseph K. makes a **cold call** or calls a prospect on the phone. *"In this case, I at least use the opportunity to tell the prospect quickly what it's all about. That almost always works and in many cases the prospect spends a few more minutes on the phone and even asks questions. Then, I know that he's interested and I schedule an appointment."*

When he makes cold calls, Joseph K. at least tries **to sound out** if the prospect may turn into a new customer. *"This usually works only in smaller businesses if I'm dealing directly with the general manager and if he is available at the time. If you're cold calling at a large company, you need more luck."*

Always inquire

Even if Joseph K. doesn't reach the desired contact, his visit is not *in vain*. *"I ask for other possible contacts or what time would be more favourable. Sometimes I'm lucky and I'm asked to return following my last appointment."* The sales representative *has determined* that *"in the late afternoons, the hurdles for cold calls are usually lower than in the mornings."*

It's *comparatively rare* for a customer to be under extreme time pressure if the appointment is a scheduled one. *"These are mostly situations that nobody could have foreseen,"* explains Joseph K. Once, while visiting an important customer, the sales talk was constantly interrupted because things had *gone haywire* at the customer's branch office. In this case, the customer was very relieved when Joseph K. offered *to postpone* the talk. *"Two days later, I visited him again around noon. On this occasion he took a lot of time and invited me out to lunch. Afterwards I was able to take my time in introducing my offer to him which he accepted without any major changes."*

Palabras para recordar

to be pressed for time: to be pressed for time: to be short of, have barely enough, or too little time

disadvantage: drawback, snag, downside, handicap, liability, obstacle

to judge: to assess, to evaluate, to perceive, to recognise, to comprehend

to seize: to grab, to take hold of, to take advantage of

to act: to proceed, to operate, to work

according to: in line with, in keeping with, following, in conformity with

to be in a hurry: to be rushed, to have little or no time

(continúa)

Continuación

to be easily cajoled: to be talked into something with no trouble

to be annoyed: to be angry, frustrated, displeased, bothered, or exasperated

to be aware of the fact: to be conscious of or sensitive to the reality

to pay dearly for something: to be punished for or atone for something

to throw someone off: to take someone unawares or by surprise

to not beat about the bush: to get down to business immediately

to express: to state, to say, to voice

distinctly: precisely, plainly

to envision: to envisage, to picture

to make flimsy excuses: to make feeble, weak, poor, or thin pretences

outside supplier: subcontractor, component supplier

cold call: unannounced visit at a prospective customer's company

to sound out: to investigate, to explore, to examine, to probe

in vain: futile, unsuccessful, unavailing

has determined: has found out, learned, experienced, or discovered

comparatively rare: relatively infrequent, few and far between, or uncommon

to foresee: to anticipate, to predict

to go haywire: to go wrong, to go out of control, to become disorganised

to postpone: to defer, to reschedule

major: bigger, greater

Profiting from refusals

Each refusal *induce you to re-evaluate* and further optimise your acquisition strategy. When doing so, *take* the following points into *consideration*:

✔ The contact person

- Did you focus on the correct contact person? Was he indeed the decision maker?

- Did you identify the co-decision makers and other *influential* people in the company?

- Did you have contact with them also or were they present when sales representatives visited the company?

- Did you work your way from "top to bottom," meaning that you tried to contact the highest decision making *authority* first?

✔ *Submitting* the offer

- Were you fully *aware of* the customer's wishes and requirements before you *drew up* the offer?

- Did you *tailor* your offer to the customer's wishes and requirements?

- Did it *clearly come into play* in what way your company is especially suited to fulfill these wishes and requirements?

- What did you hear from the sales force about the presentation? Do you have accurate information regarding the customer's reaction and possible objections?

✔ The closing phase

- Did the closing phase begin at the *appropriate* time?

- Were all crucial *issues* resolved *beforehand*?

- Were the customer's *doubts* and *concerns* identified and cleared up or *removed*?

- Did the customer, *of his own accord*, show that he's ready to close?

✔ Ask why. If an offer *didn't materialise* although, from your standpoint, chances were good, it *is worthwhile* to contact the customer one more time. Doing so *provides* the following advantages:

- If the customer has not yet made a *final* decision on another supplier, your call may leave the impression of you being positive and *committed*. You're showing that the customer is important to you.

- If the customer has already made his decision *in favour of* a competitor, a call in which you offer him that he can contact you any time, also leaves a good impression –only, of course, if you behave toward the customer just as respectfully and friendly as you did before the refusal.

- If the customer decided not to make any capital investment any time soon, you may still try *to convince him to do otherwise*. But show him that you respect his decision and then wait a while before *making another attempt*. Get the customer to agree that you may contact him again at a later point in time.

Motivating yourself after a refusal

If an important project happens to be cancelled early in the morning, this is not exactly the best *prerequisite* for starting work highly motivated. The following points are to support you in your motivation *efforts*.

✔ Even though you my be very disappointed, do not give up. Think about *similar* projects that you brought to a successful close.

✔ *Let one day pass by* in order *to get over* what happened, then discuss with your colleagues how *to deal with* the refusal and whether you should contact the customer again to find out the (true) reasons for his decision.

✔ Never *regard* a refusal as something final. Keep
the option open that an order may *come about*
at a later time.

✔ Consider it a positive *challenge* to put all your
energies into finding new customers just now.
But accept the fact that there are phases in
which *merely* generating one order is extremely
difficult, while it is much easier at other times.
Practice keeping your *staying power* and do
not waver in your commitment.

The wrong customer?

Despite using qualified address material, you may
acquire a prospect who doesn't actually *match* your
target groups. The customer may be from an industry
that you are not able to serve or there may be suppliers
who fulfill his requirements better. If this *turns out to
be true*, of course there is no point in *pressing on*.

However, you should think about how *to
avoid* such situations in the future. For
example:

✔ Ask even more detailed questions about the
company and their *line of business.*

✔ Inform yourself *in depth* about the products
and solutions the prospect *employs* at present.

✔ Think about whether your products really
make good sense for the potential customer
or whether the size of his company allows for
making a capital investment of *that magnitude*.

Palabras para recordar

refusal: negative response, rejection, non-acceptance, no,
thumbs down, negation

to induce one: to provoke, prompt, inspire, or motivate one

to re-evaluate: to re-examine, to re-assess, to have
another look at

(continúa)

Continuación

to take into consideration: to take into account, to bear in mind, to remember

influential: powerful, important, high-ranking, leading

authority: expert, specialist, professional

to submit: to present, to put forward, to proffer, to hand in

to be aware of something: to be conscious of, informed of, or familiar with something

to draw up: to compose, to formulate, to write out, to put down on paper

to tailor to: to adapt, modify, or adjust to

to clearly come into play: to unmistakeably stand out, show up, or catch the eye

appropriate: right, proper, fitting, apt, opportune

issue: question, subject, matter, topic

beforehand: earlier, in advance, ahead of time, already

doubts: misgivings, qualms, worries, uncertainties, fears, suspicions

concerns: apprehensions, trepidations, worries

removed: eliminated, taken away, done away with, eradicated

of one's own accord: of one's own free, will, voluntarily, freely

to not materialise: to not occur, happen, come about, or come to pass

to be worthwhile: to be sensible, advisable, worth the effort, or useful

to provide: to present, to offer, to yield, to impart

final: definitive, definite, absolute, irrevocable

committed: dedicated, loyal, devoted, very involved

in favour of: for, in support of, on behalf of, pro

(continúa)

Continuación

to convince one to do otherwise: to persuade or influence one to reconsider

to make another attempt: to try again, to make a new effort

prerequisite: circumstance, situation, condition

effort: attempt, endeavour, try

similar: comparable, alike, much the same, related

to let one day pass by: to allow 24 hours to elapse or go by

to get over something: to think no more of or come around from something

to deal with something: to cope with, take care of, handle, or manage something

to regard: to consider, to think of, to deem, to look upon, to view

to come about: to happen, to occur, to crop up, to take place

challenge: test, trial

merely: just, only, simply, nothing more than

staying power: endurance, stamina, fortitude, patience

to not waver: to not falter, to not hesitate, to not become unsteady

to match: to fill into, to go with, to belong to

to turn out to be true: to happen to be correct, to end up being accurate

to press on: to continue to pursue, to broach the subject again, to push on

to avoid: to keep away from, to steer

line of business: area of trade, field of commerce

in depth: thoroughly, extensively, comprehensive, in detail

to employ: to work with, to use, to make use of, utilise

to make good sense: to be a good idea, practical, or useful

of that magnitude: of that scale, degree, or size

Achieving *success* in a difficult market

Competition is quite tough among home builders but Viola Christophel, franchise partner with Town & Country, *cannot complain about a lack of* orders.

To Viola Christophel from Brandenburg, who is a licensed partner of the massive construction homes builder Town & Country, clear positioning in the market is an essential *prerequisite* for success. *"We offer massive construction homes in the low-price segment. Our main target group* **consists of** *young families with average incomes."*

Because these customers have an especially high *security need*, Viola Christophel *approaches* the matter at the beginning of the sales talk. She explains to her customers that they are automatically *covered against* risks if they decide to buy a Town & Country house.

Always oriented towards the customer

This *entails* presenting to the customer a certificate with a building quality, finance, and building service cover, which is automatically included in the price. It's just as important to Viola Christophel first to determine the customer's financial *frame* and how he *envisions* his dream home.

The actual planning of the house plays an important role in the sales talk. Viola Christophel *attaches great importance to* clarifying and discussing every detail because great emotional values are attached to living in your own home: *"The customer wants to improve his quality of life and fulfill his dream."* In order to give the customer a good idea of how his dream can come true, Viola Christophel draws up a virtual model of the house on the computer, precisely matching the customer's wishes. At the end of the sales talk, the customer receives a computer print

-out of his future house, an especially important moment, as Viola Christophel emphasises. *"The customer sees his finished home in front of him. This **raises his anticipation**."* Before the customer leaves, something important must be taken care of: Agreeing on a follow-up appointment to clarify all the planning and financing details.

Proactive marketing

Intense marketing **is an integral part** of Viola Christophel's work. She **is responsible** for local marketing activities, while headquarters deals with national marketing efforts. Ad campaigns are supported by the franchise provider but Viola Christophel also **takes advantage of** being locally present, for example by **attending** local house building exhibitions and by making personal contact with potential customers.

Showing **structurally completed homes** results in many customer contacts: As part of a marketing campaign, the Town & Country customer agrees to have his house shown before completion. "The customers **are proud of** their new homes, so most of them agree to have them shown," says Viola Christophel.

Customer retention worthwhile

It is also worth one's while to follow up with customers who buy a house only once in their lifetime, emphasises Viola Christophel, because *"I get a lot of **referrals** from them."* The customers are proud of their houses and are pleased to pass their positive experiences on to others. Therefore, Viola Christophel is always able to turn to her referral customers if a potential customer wants to see a lived-in Town & Country home from the inside and exchange ideas with the home owner.

Checking out *the competition*

It's not a taboo subject for Viola Christophel that prospects also check out the competition. *"We can talk openly about that!"* While she **nudges some customers onto** the subject herself (*"Have you looked somewhere else yet?"*), other customers, referring to the competition, try **to haggle the price down** several thousand euros. In this case also, Viola Christophel has a clear strategy: *"I ask the customer to re-examine if the same services he gets from us are also included in the competitor's offer. As a rule, this is not the case."*

Palabras para recordar

to achieve: to attain, to reach, to arrive at, to gain, to earn

to not be able to complain about: to not be able to grumble, grouse, moan, or lament about

a lack of: an absence of, a deficiency in, a shortage of, a scarcity of

prerequisite: requirement, necessity, precondition

to consist of: to be made up of, to be formed of, to comprise, to contain, to include

security need: requirement, demand, or wish for safekeeping

to approach: to deal with, to tackle, to handle, to set about

to be covered against something: to be insured against, provided for, or protected against something

to entail: to involve, to require, to call for, to necessitate

frame: condition, state, situation, circumstance

to envision: to imagine, to picture, to visualise, to envisage

to attach great importance to something: to think or consider something to be essential

to raise someone's anticipation: to boost someone's joyful expectancy

(continúa)

Continuación

to be an integral part: to be a basic, fundamental, or essential element

to be responsible for: to be in charge of, accountable for, or in control of

to take advantage of something: to profit from, cash in on, or make the most of something

to attend: to be present at, to go to, to visit, to turn up at

structurally completed home: bare brickwork house, building shell

to be proud of something: to be pleased with, happy about, appreciative of, or satisfied with something

referral: recommendation, reference, good word

to check out: to look into, to take a look at, to examine, to research

to nudge someone onto something: to gently push or urge someone onto something

to haggle the price down: to bargain or negotiate for lowering the cost by

to re-examine: to reconsider, to reassess, to re-evaluate, to check again

Capítulo 4

Atender al cliente y tratar con él

· ·

En este capítulo

▶ Saber qué quieren los clientes

▶ Cómo ganarte su confianza

▶ Mantener los clientes

▶ No perder el contacto con los clientes

· ·

Primero está el vendedor, luego el producto o el servicio que se ofrece y, finalmente, la persona a quien se destina dicho producto o servicio: el cliente, tercer gran pilar de todo negocio.

De entrada, el cliente no es sino un ente abstracto que se materializará, a lo largo de nuestra carrera como vendedores, en infinidad de personalidades diferentes: el cliente serio, el desenfadado, el inseguro, el puntilloso y un largo etcétera imposible de enumerar.

En este capítulo aprenderás, entre otras muchas cosas, a tratar con todos esos clientes potenciales, a saber qué quieren y cómo debes tratarlos, y también a aprovechar sus reclamaciones y sus ideas en beneficio de tu empresa. Y recuerda esta máxima: El cliente siempre tiene la razón. Aunque eso no signifique que sea imposible hacerle cambiar de idea...

Find out what prospective customers want

"Send me something in writing" can be a potential customer's legitimate request, or *a stall to get rid of* you. Try this response, *"I will. What specifically would you like to see?"* This can be a *major* door-opener, will help determine if the prospect is *sincere*, and give you an idea of his interest level. If he can't describe what he is looking for, it is *apparent* he doesn't have a desire to see anything. If he *mentions* specifics, you might be able to answer his request by phone. *Either way*, you have a better idea of where you stand with him.

Palabras para recordar

a stall: delaying tactics, a pretext

to get rid of someone: to free or unburden oneself of someone

major: important, great, weighty, prime

sincere: honest, straightforward, plain-dealing, not deceitful

apparent: obvious, clear, evident, plain, discernible

to mention: to talk about, to bring up, to call attention to, to point out

either way: one way or another, whichever way you look at it, somehow or other

---

Being present without pressuring

Salespeople who *put their customers under pressure* and *push them* to make the buying decision, *attain* only short-term success, if any at all.

It's much more likely that the customer will not buy in the first place or *regrets* his purchase afterwards.

Sales experts agree: One of the most important success factors for sales representatives is their presence with the customer. This *applies especially to* acquiring new customers. "If you let more than 15 days go by between the initial and the follow-up appointment, you are *banished* from the customer's mind," explains Michael Weber, sales manager Germany for Viessmann, Allendorf.

More often than not, this presence with the customer *is mistaken for* applying massive pressure. Instead of showing an interest in the customer and taking his needs seriously, he is pressed towards a decision. "This starts as early as scheduling the appointment," says telephone trainer Klaus J. Fink from Bad Honnef: *"If the appointment is forced on the customer, he develops a feeling comparable to buyer's remorse."*

Offering benefit instead of applying pressure is *the most promising* way to go. On the one hand, sales representatives should allow their customers enough *free space* so they won't feel pressured but on the other hand *convey* to them that they always will be there for them and advise them competently in all important matters.

For example, it is especially beneficial to the customer, if the sales representative makes the *transition* to the new supplier as easy as possible. *"This entails*, for example, the sales representative programming all the important contact numbers into the customer's telephone system," explains Michael Weber. Moreover, conducting extensive user workshops for customers and supporting them in all technical matters are *decisive* factors in *retaining* your customers.

Palabras para recordar

to put someone under pressure: to put the screws on or hassle someone

to push someone to do something: to impel, goad, induce, or exhort someone to do something

to attain: to reach, to achieve, to accomplish, to obtain, to arrive at, to earn

to regret: to be unhappy with, to be remorseful about, to feel sorry about

to apply especially to: to be particularly relevant, pertinent, or significant to

to be banished: to be eliminated, dismissed, or removed

is mistaken for: is confused with, mixed up with, or misinterpreted as

to be forced on someone: to be pushed on someone, to be thrust down someone's throat

buyer's remorse: purchaser's regret, sorrow, or contriteness

to offer benefit: to provide advantage, to give assistance, to furnish gain

the most promising: the best, the most favourable, auspicious, or positive

free space: leeway, freedom, flexibility, room to manoeuvre

to convey: to communicate, to express, to put across, to make known, to impart

transition: change, switch, conversion, changeover, shift

this entails: this involves, requires, calls for, or necessitates

decisive: important, key, significant, crucial, critical, deciding, determining

to retain: to keep, to preserve, to keep possession of, to keep hold of

Discuss a customer's buying inhibitions *openly*

If a customer **drags out** his decision it is a sure sign that he is **struggling with** buying inhibitions.

Gerald F. has been selling luxury company cars for years. Still, it became rather difficult for him to get his customers to sign the sales contract. *"They raise all sorts of objections and ask for time to think it over. Some of them* **pretend not to be there** *when I call to find out how far they've come in making a decision."*

The way these customers behaved **caused him considerable anguish**: *"I was at a loss and didn't know what I was doing wrong. Then I began to doubt whether I was really working in the right industry."*

Finally the car salesman tried a different strategy. *"I simply asked my customers what is keeping them from making the final decision."* Then Gerald F. found out the following: *"They want to buy but are concerned because they* **find it inappropriate** *when they're* **pushing for cost saving measures** *in their companies and then show up with a new luxury car."*

Since he knows about this buying inhibition, it has become much easier for Gerald F. to come up with suitable arguments during his sales talks. *"I convince my customers that they are not* **only entitled to** *a luxury car but by driving it they* **exude** *success and* **convey** *security to their staff and customers."*

Thorough analysis

Even in the **capital goods** business, where normally only hard facts and figures matter, salespeople are struggling with **unspoken** buying inhibitions. Sales engineer Helmut K. from Hannover has no illusions about potential risks. *"Initially, one is quite confident that there is nothing to stop the closing and suddenly*

*you are dealt a blow: The customer **declines**
without further explanation."*

Therefore, the sales engineer **has gotten into the
habit of** watching for possible buying inhibitions
from the beginning of the acquisition process. By
taking a close look at the customer's company
and the customer's behaviour, he can **assess** what
type of customer he is dealing with. If he is still not
ready **to draw a conclusion** from this, he asks a
few seemingly insignificant questions in order to
determine which buying reservation he has to be
prepared for.

Picking up signals

*"A couple of weeks ago, for example, I visited a
customer whose visitors' room **was furnished with**
a **faded corner seating unit** and **closets** from the
70s. It **dawned on me** immediately: If the customer
is that **miserly**, an old machine must be completely
unserviceable before he decides to purchase a new
one."* Helmut K. based his sales strategy on this
estimation. *"First we talked about today's high **wages**
and **utility costs**. Then we wondered how we could
force them down in order to reduce production costs.
Now I was able **to bring my machine into play**.
I explained to the customer how he could make money
selling his old machine and lower costs and increase
profits by purchasing a new one."*

Helmut K. has to deal with tight-fisted customers
not nearly as often as with **anxious ones**. Such
customers quickly **give themselves away**. *"You
detect their worries in every question and answer. They
are afraid they will **overextend themselves** if they buy
the machine or that they can't operate or make correct
use of it."* In order to be completely sure what keeps
customers from buying, the sales representative
directly addresses the **supposed reason** for not
buying. *"In using examples and facts, I make it clear
to the customer that his reservations **are completely
unfounded**."*

Palabras para recordar

inhibition: reservations, qualms, hesitancy, doubt, restraint

to drag out: to protract, to prolong, to draw out, to delay, to stretch out, to extend

to struggle with something: to try to come to grips or deal with something

to pretend not to be there: to feign or simulate that one is not present

to cause one considerable anguish: to trigger a great deal of suffering or distress in one

to be at a loss: to be at one's wit's end, to be baffled, perplexed, or puzzled

to find it inappropriate: to think of it as improper, tasteless, unseemly, unfitting, or tactless

to push for cost-saving measures: to enforce a cost-cutting or belt-tightening course of action

to be entitled to something: to be given the right or be qualified to have something

to exude: to radiate, to give off, to emanate, to display, to show

to convey: to express, to communicate, to suggest, to put across

capital goods: investment or industrial commodities

unspoken: undeclared, unsaid, unexpressed, not spelled out

one is dealt a blow: one experiences a setback, disappointment, misfortune, or knock-back

to decline without further explanation: to say no without giving a reason

to have gotten into the habit of doing something: to have started a routine or practice of doing something

(continúa)

Continuación

to assess: to judge, to determine, to weigh up, to rate, to evaluate

to draw a conclusion: to deduce, infer, conclude, derive, or gather something

to be furnished with: to be outfitted or fitted out with

faded: dull, pale, discoloured, washed out

corner seating unit: sitting area, lounge suite, settee arrangement, three-piece suite

closet: cabinet, cupboard

to dawn on one: to occur to one, to register with one, to enter or cross one's mind

miserly: tight-fisted, penny-pinching, stingy, closefisted, parsimonious, tight, ungenerous

unserviceable: useless, worthless, inadequate, ineffective

wage: salary, earnings, income, take-home pay, remuneration

utility costs: expenses for electricity, gas, water

to force something down: to cut, lower, or reduce something

to bring something into play: to bring something up, to start talking about something

anxious ones: worried, concerned, fearful, apprehensive, uneasy, or nervous ones

to give oneself away: to reveal, divulge, or make known oneself

to detect: to notice, to perceive, to identify, to become aware of, to sense

Remain friendly regardless

Blows below the belt and frustrations are part of the salesperson's profession. Yet true professionals can handle these things in a productive manner.

In the beginning of his career, sales representative Peter K. lived through a number of frustrating situations, where he felt like ***throwing in the towel***. He credits his ***perseverance***, for the most part, to his mentor, an older colleague, who ***accompanied*** him to his first customer visits. *"He taught me that, even after the lowest blow, you have to show up at your next customer's doorstep like nothing happened."* The most important rules that were ***impressed upon*** Peter K. by his mentor:

✔ As a sales representative, you have to be prepared for almost anything; even that each and every one of the customer talks may ***play out*** differently from what you planned. When you ***adapt to*** this, you will not waste your energy by ***fretting about*** it.

✔ A salesperson has to accept and value his customers just as they are, including their ***idiosyncrasies*** and ***quirks***. Only when the customer can feel this positive attitude towards him, the right basis for doing business together is created.

✔ Deals that ***fell through*** will only then become ***failures*** if the salesperson gets frustrated about them and takes this anger out on the other customers.

✔ A sales pro always ***keeps his composure***, no matter how he actually feels inside at that particular moment. He is even capable of positively influencing his own mood through this ***exterior*** discipline.

✔ A good salesperson thinks of the customer first. Only those salespeople who focus too much on themselves are commonly in a bad mood.

> ✔ When in doubt, always smile *pleasantly* and never allow yourself to get into a confrontation. Whoever remains friendly has a much better chance of *getting one's way*.

Another trick that helps Peter K. to be consistently friendly to his customers, *"I keep reminding myself how much money I'm earning with the help of these customers and how little it costs me to be nice to them."*

Palabras para recordar

regardless: anyway, in any case, nevertheless, nonetheless, despite everything, no matter what

blows below the belt: letdowns, setbacks, failures

to throw in the towel: to resign, to quit, to give up, to walk away, to capitulate

perseverance: persistence, determination, resoluteness, insistence, tenacity

to accompany: to go along with, to go together with, to escort

to impress upon someone: to emphasise to, instil in, or bring home to someone

to play out: to develop, to proceed, to progress, to advance, to ensue

to adapt to: to become accustomed to, to get a feel for, to get used to

to fret about something: to worry about, make a fuss over, or feel peeved about something

idiosyncrasy: peculiarity, individual trait, habit

quirk: foible, oddity, hang-up, eccentricity

to fall through: to come to nothing, to go awry, to fizzle out

failure: defeat, fiasco, blunder, shortfall, flop, loss

(continúa)

Continuación

to keep one's composure: to keep a stiff upper lip, one's poise, or one's self-possession

exterior: outward, outer, external

pleasantly: in a friendly way, politely, agreeably, in a charming way, amiably

to get one's way: to prevail, to come out on top, to get others to agree

The "Magic Six" for good customer rapport

Most of the time, it will be *the really self-evident things* that *give you that edge to appeal to* customers. Yet, sometimes even the minimum requirements *cannot be maintained* in the hectic daily routine.

However, six criteria should always be present, no matter whether you are talking to your customer on the phone or in person:

- ✔ Friendliness.
- ✔ *Dependability*.
- ✔ Competence.
- ✔ *Promptness*.
- ✔ Flexibility.
- ✔ *Accessibility*.

Palabras para recordar

rapport: understanding, affinity, harmony

the really self-evident things: the things that go without saying, the most natural things

(continúa)

Continuación

to give one that edge: to provide one with the advantage or upper hand

to appeal to someone: to go down well with someone, to attract someone

cannot be maintained: cannot be upheld, kept up, or preserved

dependability: reliability, loyalty, steadiness, steadfastness, constancy

promptness: speediness, rapidity, swiftness, quickness

accessibility: attainability, availability

Do all customers deserve equal treatment?

Value-oriented customer management *requires* that there be a *clear distinction* between key account management and the activities of *overall sales*.

In *genuine*, value-oriented customer care, it is impossible to give every customer the same treatment. Intensity and strategic focus of the costumer contact *depend upon* the customer's contribution to the company. A *clearly defined boundary* between key account management and servicing less profitable customers does more than save costs because customers with *low profit contribution* don't need to be cared for so elaborately by the sales representatives. It also *eases* the work burden of qualified sales professionals because they are now able to concentrate their efforts on profitable key accounts.

The following steps are targeted towards *accomplishing* a clear separation of key account management from overall sales

✔ ***Determining*** the concurrence between the key account's requirements and the products offered.

✔ Analysing one's own ***standing*** with the key account's decision makers and influencers, and examining the key account's estimation of the products.

✔ Examining the prospective key account's willingness to cooperate – most of all: how far-reaching the collaboration can be (customer integration).

✔ ***Determining*** the three most important selling arguments for the key account.

✔ Researching and filtering out industry trends ***in accordance with*** the selling arguments in order to increase sales opportunities.

✔ Analysing the key account's decision makers; once again coordination and individualisation of the sales arguments.

✔ Communicating the key account management's strategic objective to the sales team and ***deepening*** it.

✔ ***Drawing up*** short and middle-term plans for action and ***differentiate*** between positive as well as negative decisions and measures (How to go about approaching the prospective key account? What must be avoided?)

The international management consultancy, Miller Heiman, recommends to first closely analyse the competitive situation from the key account's point of view and to develop separate sales argumentations and strategies. This view is also supported by sales expert Peter Winkelmann.

Absolute musts for key account management in the industrial goods industry are: providing individual care, separating **responsibility** for **turnover** and results in sales, and developing **joint** projects (so-called customer integration).

In an assessment for the University of St. Gallen, Uwe May, general manager for the consultant firm Maihiro, explains, *"**Within the realm** of value-oriented key account management, different product and service packages should also **be compiled** for the customers according to their significance."* Customer service that makes a distinction between key accounts and less profitable customers could look like this:

✔ Personal support service by one sales representative: only key accounts.

✔ Personal support service by the call centre: only key accounts and the more profitable customers.

A distinction is also made in the handling of complaints: While less profitable customers merely receive standardised complaint care, a customer service representative is **assigned specifically to attend** to the key accounts' complaints.

Palabras para recordar

to deserve equal treatment: to be worthy of one and the same handling

to require: to demand, to necessitate, to entail, to involve

a clear distinction: an explicit dividing line, separation, or differentiation

overall sales: general or total selling

genuine: real, authentic, true, valid

to depend upon: to be contingent upon, subject to, determined by, based on, or influenced by

a clearly defined boundary: a plainly marked out, established, or settled demarcation line

(continúa)

Continuación

low profit contribution: scarce contribution margin, product profitability, or profit margin

to ease: to relieve, to reduce, to lessen

responsibility: liability, accountability, answerability

turnover: gross revenue, volume of business

joint: common, shared, combined, collective, cooperative, consolidated, concerted

within the realm: within the framework, scheme, system, area, or field

to be compiled: to be assembled, put together, or brought together

to be assigned specifically: to be appointed, allocated, designated, or named purposefully

to attend to: to take care of, to handle, to deal with, to give one's attention to

to accomplish: to achieve, to get done, to realise, to bring about

to determine: to ascertain, to establish, to verify, to clarify

standing: status, position, reputation, rank

to determine: to find out, to reveal, to uncover

in accordance with: in agreement, conformity, or compliance with

to deepen: to intensify, to reinforce, to emphasize, to stress, to underline

to draw up: to formulate, to work out, to create, to think up, to devise

to differentiate: to distinguish, to make a distinction, to contrast

Establishing stable *customer* relationships

Sales representatives, who manage *to win over* their customers not only on a business but also on a personal level, are creating a good basis for their customer relationships.

Sales representatives, who do *not regard* their customers *merely* as income producers but show an honest interest in them, have a greater chance for doing long-term, successful business with them.

"The personal, human bond often decides whether you can hold a customer or not," reports a sales representative who works for a *spare parts wholesaler* in the automobile industry. In his opinion, the way you *treat* your customers *counts more than* a low price. *"The customer has to feel that it's not about just making a quick sale but it's about* **appreciating** *and respecting him on a personal level."* To the sales representative, it is important that the customer feels comfortable in his *presence* and *has trust in him*. *"This is easy to recognise, because the customer talks about personal matters or tells me 'Well, then you don't see your family all week,' or something like it."*

Matters become somewhat difficult if the customer is *fixated on* the sales representative's persona. *"Some customers want me to take care of every* **minor detail***, even if it's really the interior sales force's job,"* says the sales representative. So not *to snub* his A customers, he takes care of them *virtually* by himself. *"However, if I'm dealing with a new customer, I try to be clear about who is playing what role."*

Personal *connection*

Sales coach Helmut Seßler from Mannheim advises sales representatives to always look for what they *have in common with* their customers and thus create a personal connection. There may be all kinds of things you and your customers have in common. Some typical examples: You realise that your children are the same age, you worked *previously* in the same region, you *recently* saw the same musical, you have the same hobby, etc. Even negative experiences can make you bond, *provided* you can discuss them with humour.

Palabras para recordar

stable: solid, strong, long-lasting, secure, steady, firm

to win over: to bring around, to persuade, to prevail upon, to influence

to not regard: to not look upon, consider, see, deem, or think of

merely: just, only, simply, purely

spare parts wholesaler: extra or replacement component trader

to treat: to act toward, to behave toward, to deal with, to handle

to count more than: to matter more, be more important or significant than

to appreciate: to value, to think highly of, to hold in high esteem

presence: being there, company

to have trust in someone: to have faith, confidence, or belief in someone

to be fixated on someone: to be preoccupied or engrossed with someone

(continúa)

Continuación

minor detail: inconsequential, insignificant, or trivial circumstance

to snub: to affront, to offend, to upset, to insult, to slight

virtually: practically, nearly, almost, as good as, essentially

connection: link, association, bond

to have in common with someone: to do or experience similarly as someone

previously: formerly, earlier on, in the past, before, once, at one time

recently: just, a short time ago, lately

to bond: to connect, to get on, to hit it off, to get along

provided: as long as, if, given, with the provision that, on the condition that

Gain your customers' respect

If salespeople *are put to the test* by their customers, only one thing helps: to win their respect through competence.

Sales visits may be doubly difficult for junior sales representatives. On the one hand, they may *be lacking* the necessary routine to be in complete control of the sales talks. On the other hand, they may be put to the test by their customers. *"Customers test to see if you're a match for them,"* Manfred Reitinger, a technical sales representative for the Fuchs Austria Schmiermittel (Lubricant) GmbH in Bergheim, Austria, remembers his career start. *"They weighed every one of my words and asked questions that were intended to provoke me. Some of the customers behaved downright condescending and arrogant."*

To Manfred Reitinger, such customer visits **were comparable to running the gauntlet.** "*I was constantly worried* about saying a **thoughtless** word and always lived in fear of doing something wrong."

Inside the customer's world

Today, Manfred Reitinger is as comfortable in his job as a fish in water. The customers who used to put him to the test now **appreciate** his **advice** and trust his high competence. In this process, neither they nor Reitinger have changed.

Only the situation has changed. "**Back then**, I didn't belong to the customers' world but today I'm **part of it**," says Manfred Reitinger. His selling **achievements prove** how very much he is integrated today, making him Fuchs Austria's Salesman of the Year.

Fight for trust

It may take a while before customers let you be part of their industry world. Reitinger knows why, "*especially in a technical industry like ours, customers want **to play it safe**. They have to be certain that a supplier or sales representative keeps his promises.*"

Manfred Reitinger has created this basis of trust. His most important rule is: *Only say what you really know and only promise what you can really keep.*

If you **adhere to** this rule you can count on your customers' support. "*They don't expect from a first-time sales representative that he can do and know everything,*" says Reitinger. However, they have to sense that the sales representative does everything in his power to do his work good and right. "*Then it may **occur** that a beginner **is taken under his customer's wing** and helped over the first steps.*"

Build up competences

The beginner's bonus lasts only during the first weeks and months.

Manfred Reitinger knew that his customers' tolerance would *be exhausted relatively soon* and it was important to him to build up *extensive* competences as quickly as possible. By taking advantage of in-house qualifying measures, his industry's trade media, and discussions with experts he created a broad basis for his expert knowledge. Even today he systematically improves this know-how, because *"in my industry you can never know enough."*

Manfred Reitinger has long since lost the *inhibitions* of the first months when he advises an experienced production manager about the *utilization* of his lubrication products. He quickly gains the respect of new customers when he *convincingly* presents his products' benefits and when he knows how to deal with *objections*, thrown in by the negotiation partners, by presenting *sound* arguments, figures, and facts *to refute* them.

Even during difficult negotiations, Manfred Reitinger *remains unflappable* because the arguments with which he refutes his customers' objections are part of his experiences gathered during the course of his professional life.

Palabras para recordar

to be put to the test: to be tested, assessed, evaluated, or scrutinised

to be lacking: to not have, to be short of, to be deficient in

to be a match for someone: to be an equal, an equivalent, or a peer for someone

to weigh every word: to judge, assess, or contemplate each remark

(continúa)

Continuación

downright: blatantly, utterly, completely, totally, absolutely, out-and-out

condescending: patronising, snobbish

to be comparable to: to be like, equivalent to, or similar to

to run the gauntlet: being critically and unsympathetically observed by a group of people

to be constantly worried: to be always anxious, nervous, or concerned

thoughtless: unthinking, unmindful, unwise, heedless, careless

to appreciate: to value, to hold in high regard, to respect

advice: counsel, guidance, opinion

back then: in those early days, in those former times

to be part of something: to be associated with or involved in something

achievement: success, accomplishment, feat

to prove: to show, to verify, to confirm, to demonstrate, to attest

to play it safe: to be on the safe side, to be out of harm's way

to adhere to: to stick to, to abide by, to comply with

to occur: to happen, to come about, to come to pass

to be taken under someone's wing: to be protected, looked after, or watched over by someone

to be exhausted soon: to be used up, finished, or depleted before long

extensive: comprehensive, wide-ranging, thorough

inhibitions: reserve, hang-ups, shyness, self-consciousness

utilization: use, usage, handling

(continúa)

Continuación

convincingly: persuasively, credibly, believably, compellingly

objection: counterargument, opposition

sound: solid, well-founded, well-grounded, concrete, valid

to refute: to disprove, to counter, to contest, to rebut

to remain unflappable: to stay in control, composed, level-headed, self-possessed, or collected

Handling difficult customers

In everyday selling, the following types of customers may *cause you a lot of grievance*. We show you how to deal with them *skilfully*:

The changer

This type of customer turns everything you say around and reinterprets it, in part *unintentionally*, because he misunderstands something and in part intentionally in order *to corner you*, for example, to get a price reduction.

Corrective measure:

If you're dealing with such a customer, sentences such as *"We will look into that and let you know"* are helpful. In this situation, it is also very important to send a brief e-mail after the phone conversation to document in writing what has been discussed.

The worrier

This customer calls all the time (or has someone else call for him), takes a very long time to come to a decision, and after placing

the order asks worriedly if everything is really OK.

Corrective measure:

Remind the customer, if possible, of former business transactions with your company that ***went off without a hitch***. If you're dealing with a first-time customer, call him a few times ***of your own accord to reassure him*** that his order is being taken care of and that he is in good hands. This will help ***calm him down***.

The nit-picker

You need ***to be especially on guard*** with him because this type of customer will even be able ***to memorise the fine print***. Moreover, he will tell you how ***much more favourable*** the competitor's offer is.

Corrective measure:

In this situation, ***to remain matter-of-fact*** is the top priority. If, for example, the customer tries ***to bad-mouth*** your company's service, get to the bottom of the matter by asking him for concrete details as to why he objects.

The innocent victim

This customer ***alleges*** that something was promised to him that no one in your company could ever fulfill or influence.

Corrective measure:

Put the cards on the table and speak openly and honestly with this customer. Make it clear what you cannot fulfill and then make a point of telling the customer concretely what your company can do for him.

Palabras para recordar

to cause one a lot of grievance: to bring one a great deal of distress or anguish

skilfully: expertly, competently, capably

unintentionally: accidentally, inadvertently, not deliberately, unintended

to corner one: to trap one, to pin one down, to back one into a corner

worrier: a person who is concerned that something bad might happen

to go off without a hitch: to go smoothly, to go without difficulties

of one's own accord: of one's own free will, voluntarily, freely, willingly

to reassure someone: to set someone's mind at rest

to calm someone down: to pacify, soothe, or appease someone

nit-picker: faultfinder, knocker, whiner

to be especially on guard: to be extra alert, vigilant, or watchful

to memorise the fine print: to remember or learn by heart the small lettering

to be much more favourable: to be much better, to be much more beneficial

to remain matter-of-fact: to stay factual, down to earth, or unemotional

to bad-mouth something: to speak critically or harshly of something

innocent victim: a person who pretends to have been wronged

to allege: to claim, to assert, to charge

How to keep customer relationships alive

Even the best of customer relationships may *fizzle out* if you don't *recharge* them from time to time.

Sales representatives usually spend a lot of time and effort in *wooing* potential customers. Once they become loyal customers, it's often just a matter of time before one starts *to neglect* them, *believing* that everything *is fine and dandy*. But every customer relationship needs to be *nurtured* and kept alive. The "closer" you stay to your customers, the quicker you find out if their requirements change or if they *contemplate* changing to a different supplier.

Call your customers off and on, even if you don't have anything to sell them at the moment. These contacts between actual sales *are suited for* giving new stimulus to the customer relationship. Always a good reason for calling is to ask the customer how satisfied he is with your products and whether they *function without a hitch*, etc. Perhaps you may *"catch"* a customer having a problem and telling you *"I'm really glad you are calling…"*

How often you contact your customers depends, on the one hand, on the buying intervals, but also, how important the individual customer is and how profitable he is for your company.

Make it a point to personally contact every one of your customers at least once or twice per year, *independent of* the usual occasions like Christmases or birthdays.

Palabras para recordar

to keep something alive: to keep something thriving, active, or blooming

to fizzle out: to peter out, to fade away, to come to an end, to disappear

to recharge: to refresh, to revitalise, to revive

to woo someone: to court, pursue, or seek to win someone

to neglect: to fail to look after, to be lax about, to pay little or no attention to

believing: thinking, supposing, being of the opinion, assuming

to be fine and dandy: to be all right, satisfactory, OK, or good

to be nurtured: to be attended to, cultivated, cared for, or looked after

to contemplate: to consider, to plan, to think about, to intend, to give thought to

to be suited for something: to be right, appropriate, or suitable for something

to function without a hitch: to run smoothly or trouble-free

to catch: to encounter, to come across, to come upon

independent of: regardless of, notwithstanding, irrespective of

Inspire and motivate customers

Only when you *are truly convinced of* and enthusiastic about your products, will you *appear credible* to your customers.

Sales pros have long realised that customers will decide not only from a *purely* rational

Four *key* factors that help to explain whether customers are motivated to buy

1. Clarity and understanding

It is necessary to be a clear contract between sales representative and customer about what they both want from the relationship. If the buyer understands your motives because you are open and *sincere*, they are more likely to trust you.

2. Expressing opinions, hopes, ideas, and *concerns*

We all have a desire *to share* our thoughts and feelings and to believe that the other person is really listening to what we have to say. This is also a matter of the salesperson asking good questions. Trust is an important factor and if the customer feels more comfortable, he is more likely to trust your *judgement* and know-how.

3. Having a choice in decisions

This *emphasises* the need for the customer to still feel in control of the buying process and one way to do that is to give the buyer a limited range of choices. The customer needs to feel involved in the decision and takes *ownership*.

4. Feeling *valued* and *recognised*

You know that your customer is important but do you make him feel important to you? Make sure that you listen carefully to what they say (no matter how many times you may have heard a similar story) and thank them.

standpoint but from an emotional one as well. That is why you should always *consider* this subjective aspect. Aside from the emotional value of a product, the relationship with you, the sales force and your company influence the customer, too.

Consequently, a friendly phone conversation with you can *tip the scales* and make the customer buy. Inspiring and motivating customers is not that difficult. Here are some examples:

✔ Customers like hearing you agree with them and **affirming** them in their considerations. When a customer says, for example, *"I would like that"* or *"this fits well,"* then you can support him. Encourage your customer **to treat himself to something** (*"You really **deserve** this"* or *"This is truly our top product."*)

✔ **Paint a clear picture of** how well your customer will feel once he **possess** and **utilises** the product. The customer has to be able **to envision in his mind** how he handles the product.

✔ Tell anecdotes and little stories about other customers and product users that will **attest** to the customer that he is making an excellent buying choice.

✔ If you are also using this particular product, tell your customer how well you like it and that you would buy it again **in an instant**. Explain the advantages you have by owning it.

✔ In case you would like to own the product but cannot, for example **due to** technical, respectively practical or financial reasons, let the customer know this as well. Congratulate him on **owning** this product soon.

Palabras para recordar

to be truly convinced of something: to be really positive, confident, certain, or sure about something

to appear credible: to seem believable, trustworthy, convincing, or sincere

purely: simply, just, solely, entirely, completely, totally, wholly

to consider: to think about, to give thought to, to ponder, to contemplate, to bear in mind

(continúa)

Continuación

to tip the scales: to have a major influence on the outcome of a situation

to affirm: to confirm, to endorse, to support, to uphold

to treat oneself to something: to indulge, spoil, or pamper oneself

to deserve: to be worthy of, to be entitled to, to have the right to, to qualify for

to paint a clear picture of something: to delineate, define, describe, outline, or portray something

to possess: to be the owner of, to hold, to take into possession, to have, to enjoy

to utilise: to use, to put to use, to employ, to handle

to envision in one's mind: to visualise, picture, or foresee in one's thinking

to attest: to authenticate, to prove, to confirm, to certify, to ratify, to validate

in an instant: instantly, at once, in no time, directly, right away, promptly

due to: because of, by reason of, on account of

to own: to be the owner of, to have possession of, to possess, to have

key: crucial, vital, critical, decisive, important, influential, significant

sincere: genuine, true, honest, unfeigned, unaffected, wholehearted, heartfelt, serious, earnest

concerns: fear, apprehension, worry, unease, trepidation, disquiet

to share: to communicate, to let somebody in on, to reveal, to disclose, to impart

judgement: common sense, good sense, perception, wisdom, understanding

(continúa)

Continuación

to emphasise: to accentuate, to call attention to, to highlight, to give prominence to, to stress

ownership: possession, control, command

valued: esteemed, highly regarded, respected, cherished, treasured

recognised: appreciated, honoured, applauded, endorsed

From satisfied to enthusiastic

Not every customer talks openly about it if something is *bothering* him. Therefore, salespeople have to be proactive to *ensure* that their customers are not just satisfied but enthusiastic about their products or services.

Salespeople who *trust* that their customers are satisfied as long as they don't complain are taking a high risk. In many cases, the *loss* of a customer does not happen over night but *has been a long time coming*. If non-communication continues, it may happen that the customer changes over to a competitor *unnoticed*.

The results are quite different for salespeople who are pro-active and make sure that such a situation does *not arise* in the first place:

✔ They are contacting their customers on a regular basis. This way they find out early on if there may be any *discrepancies*.

✔ They visit the customer to find out if he is really satisfied. For example, they talk to the users of their product, give them tips, and ask for honest feedback.

✔ They *are extremely sensitive* and *perceive* even the smallest of signals. If they have a feeling that something is not right, they speak to their customer about it.

✔ Even if complaints are *minor*, they inform customer service *to take action* by examining, repairing, or exchanging the product immediately.

✔ In regard to after-sales services, they are *tremendously accommodating* because they know that this is exactly where they can *score with* their customer.

✔ They *monitor* each *measure* they initiated and are only satisfied when the customer is *thrilled*.

Palabras para recordar

to bother: to concern, to perturb, to worry, to disconcert, to distress

to ensure: to make sure, to make certain, to guarantee

to trust: to believe, to expect, to hope

loss: leaving, departure, disappearance

to have been a long time coming: to have been in the offing for an extended period

unnoticed: unobserved, unseen, without being seen

to not arise: to not come up, occur, happen, develop, or come to pass

discrepancy: inconsistency, incongruity, difference, disagreement

to be extremely sensitive: to have keen senses, to be very receptive

to perceive: to recognise, to distinguish, to make out, to identify

minor: small, insignificant, negligible

(continúa)

Continuación

to take action: to do something, to proceed, to take steps, to get busy, to react

to be tremendously accommodating: to be exceptionally obliging or cooperative

to score with someone: to make an impression or be a hit with someone

to monitor: to keep an eye on, to keep track of, to check, to oversee

measure: step, action, move

to be thrilled: to be delighted, especially pleased, or very enthusiastic

Capítulo 5

Relaciones interpersonales y red de contactos

*E*s probable que toda relación cliente-empresa termine algún día. Por ese motivo para un negocio resulta imprescindible mantener una completa red de contactos que pueda generar nuevos posibles clientes, bien para que la empresa aumente sus beneficios o bien para sustituir a antiguos clientes sin que los beneficios se resientan.

No es una tarea fácil conseguir nuevos contactos, pero una buena organización y una buena estrategia facilitarán llegar a esa tierra prometida, a esa fuente de la eterna juventud que todo negocio persigue. ¡Suerte en la búsqueda!

Establishing and nurturing useful contacts

Good contacts *are indispensable* for sales representatives. Building up a functioning network takes a lot of initiative.

"In our industry, nothing works if you don't know the right people," explains Richard C., a sales representative for a *construction equipment* company. Knowing the right people, in other words networking, is the establishment and nurturing of personal contacts in order to build up an extensive relationship network that one *is able to access* in every situation.

However, before you can *reap* the fruits of the network, you first have to invest in it, emphasises sales representative Henry K., *"You can't expect to get support and valuable tips from others if you aren't ready to contribute your share."* In the opinion of Henry K., the benefits he *derives from* his network are great. For example, because of the support of some of his contacts he was able *to gain* access to decision makers and potential customers. *"Of course it's especially helpful if someone recommends me,"* explains the sales representative. He suggests, however, not *to limit yourself to* the obviously attractive contacts, *"because seemingly insignificant acquaintances may turn out to be quite fruitful."*

One thing *imperative* to Henry K. is to nurture his relationships. *"It's not enough to exchange business cards,"* he says. *"You have to be present for each other as human beings."* Therefore, the sales representative *made it a habit to enter* each contact's data in his organiser and to update it with additional information. *"Just like writing a call report, I note the reason for the meeting, what we talked about, what I found out about the person and when I plan to contact him or her again."* These follow-up contacts often take place on the very next day. *"Then I call again and thank him or her for the pleasant talk because my goal is to stay in contact."*

Palabras para recordar

to nurture: to cultivate, to develop, to support, to boost, to advance

to be indispensable: to be crucial, vital, essential, very important, or key

construction equipment: building tools or gear

to be able to access: to be able to get into, gain access to, or fall back on

to reap: to harvest, to bring in, to take in

to contribute one's share: to do one's bit, to play one's part

to derive from: to get, gain, receive, or draw from

to gain: to get, to win, to obtain

to limit oneself to: to restrict or confine oneself to

seemingly: apparently, outwardly, ostensibly

insignificant: unimportant, irrelevant, uninfluential, powerless

acquaintances: associates, connections, contacts

imperative: very important, vital, crucial, essential

to exchange: to swap, to trade, to barter

to make it a habit: to make it a rule, routine, or pattern

to enter: to record, to register, to put down, to note

call report: sales representative's account or description of a visit to the customer

How to deal with a new contact person

Sales business is people business and that is why it may be a ***turning point*** in business relations if your ***trusted*** contact person ***leaves*** the customer's company.

In order to avoid complications you should ***consider*** the following principles:

✔ No ***prejudices***.

Always keep in mind that the new contact person, too, had his ***steady*** and familiar contact partners at his old work place. He may be sorry for having to leave them behind and now wants to establish new personal contacts.

✔ Send welcome greetings.

By letter or by postcard. If possible, the note should be handwritten but should in no case contain any kind of ***sales pitch***. The advantage: Especially during the first weeks on the new job, the customer's new staff member will receive very little mail addressed directly to him. He will, therefore, remember your personal welcome note.

✔ ***Gather*** information about the new contact person.

If you know other people in the customer's company there is an opportunity, with their help, to find out more about the new contact person.

✔ Call him during the first few days.

Even before the customer's new staff member ***has fully adjusted to*** the change, call him ***to congratulate him*** on his new position and explain to him briefly the basis on which cooperation took place in the past. In addition, schedule an appointment for an ***"exploratory talk"*** of a ***predetermined duration*** of about 20 minutes.

Palabras para recordar

turning point: crossroads, critical period, decisive point

trusted: familiar, close, trustworthy, reliable

to leave: to give up or quit one's job at

to consider: to bear in mind, to take into account, to remember

prejudice: prejudgement, preconception, bias, predisposition

steady: regular, usual, customary, habitual

sales pitch: push, plug, or advertisement for a product or service

to gather: to collect, to get together, to accumulate

to have fully adjusted to something: to have entirely gotten used or attuned to something

to congratulate someone: to compliment or offer good wishes to someone

exploratory talk: fact-finding or investigative conversation

predetermined duration: fixed, prearranged, or preset period

New contacts can open up new opportunities

A new contact person in a customer's company can provide a big chance. It *is crucial* that you call on him or her *at an early stage*.

When Wolfgang F., a sales representative for an office service supplier, phoned some of his customers after a holiday leave he *was in for a surprise*: A long-time contact, one

of his first customers actually, ***alerted him to*** the fact that he was about to leave his current employer and would only ***be engaged in*** the company business for another few weeks. He also informed him that he would most certainly recommend the supplier to his ***replacement*** – this however proved to be of little ***comfort*** to Wolfgang F. *"I have **witnessed** time and again that a new contact has quite different views and ideas and wants to handle things differently than his **predecessor**. In addition, the competition does not rest and should they be acting quickly, there is a chance that the customer may change the supplier."*

Talk to each other without delay

Wolfgang F. ***happened to be fortunate*** with the ***aforementioned*** customer. *"I gave the new contact person two weeks time **to get accustomed to** his new **surroundings**, then I called him."* In the past, he had found it ***sufficient*** to send a letter, *"but then, I discovered that it is more favourable to introduce myself over the phone. You will then quickly know what sort of person you are dealing with, what views he has and whether he likes **to endeavour on** new ventures promptly or whether he still needs some time **to settle into his new job**."* According to his findings, Wolfgang F. either arranges a meeting straight away or at a later point in time. *"In any case, it is imperative to remain in contact."*

However, according to Wolfgang F., one should not let too much time pass before acquiring new orders. *"At any rate, I try during the first phone call to set up a meeting or at least a specific calendar week in which we will meet face-to-face."*

Observe the business environment

A face-to-face visit is quite ***revealing*** to Wolfgang F., mainly because he can gain insight into what kind of relationship *"the new guy"* has with his fellow employees. *"It is important for me to see whether he is accepted straight away or viewed somewhat suspiciously and whether he is able to sell his ideas well."* And certainly his assistant and co-workers are a good source of information. *"Even if they **contain themselves**, one can tell **on what terms they are with** their new boss."* Oftentimes, Wolfgang F. receives useful bits of information from them. *"I can learn which issues the new contact attaches importance to and how you can **impress** or inspire him."*

Palabras para recordar

to be crucial: to be decisive, essential, high-priority, or necessary

---

at an early stage: promptly, without delay, early on, ahead of schedule

---

to be in for a surprise: to experience a bolt from the blue or a revelation

---

to alert someone to something: to notify, inform, or warn someone about something

---

to be engaged in: to be involved in, to be busy with or engrossed with

---

replacement: successor, substitute, stand-in, fill-in, proxy

---

comfort: consolation, reassurance, relief, solace, help

---

to witness: to see, to observe, to watch

---

predecessor: precursor, forerunner

---

without delay: immediately, right away, at once, straight away, promptly

---

to happen to be fortunate: to turn out to be lucky or successful

(continúa)

Continuación

aforementioned: previously described, abovementioned, forenamed, aforesaid

to get accustomed to: to get used to, to become familiar with, to get adapted to

surroundings: environment, setting, milieu, situation, environs

sufficient: adequate, enough, plenty, satisfactory

to endeavour on: to try one's hand at, to do one's best at, to make an effort at

to settle into one's new job: to make oneself acquainted or familiarise oneself with one's new work

revealing: informative, enlightening, useful, helpful, educational

the new guy: the newcomer, the beginner, the new arrival

to contain oneself: to hold oneself back, to restrain oneself, to keep oneself in check, to control oneself

on what terms they are with someone: what their standing or relationship is with someone

to impress: to make an impact on, to amaze, to astonish, to stir, to influence

Networking gets you to the decision maker

Sales representatives, who from the beginning of the business relationship try to get to know all the important contacts in the customer company, increase their chances greatly for cross-selling and closing the sale.

For years, sales representative Michael O. *attended to* a good customer *without*

Find *mediators*

Some projects may go on for a long time before you make the first contact with the decision maker. In this case, it is important to establish a network of important contacts early on.

Principal mediators or coaches, as they are often called, are:

✔ People from the decision maker's private *environment* who know him well and have a trusting relationship with him. This may include the typical golf partner.

✔ People from the customer company who are working closely with the decision maker, such as his assistant and the employees who work in his department.

✔ People in the customer company who come from the same hierarchy level but *are responsible for* a different department. They could be useful as contacts because often they communicate on a collegial level and carry on a relationship on an impartial basis.

Try to win mediators and coaches, from as many directions as possible, who recommend you and who assist you in getting closer to the decision maker. First, establish personal contacts on a *semi*private or professional level (for example at trade fairs and industry events) or by telephone.

noticing that it would have been easy to generate additional business. *"The company is **divided into** individual profit centres. In the beginning I did business with only one profit centre manager who happened to be my contact, until **by chance** I got to know one of his colleagues. As it turned out, he was also interested in our solutions. Today, he is my customer and so are two other **division managers** from the same company."*

Michael O. **drew the following conclusion** from this experience: *"You have to be open to all **directions** and build a network in the customer's company."* It works out especially well if, as in his case, the contacts come from the same hierarchy level, *"then, it's not a problem for them to **introduce me to** their colleagues – they actually **enjoy doing that**."* According to Michael O., however, you should not believe that this could happen by itself or by chance. *"You have to be proactive and ask if the solution would be interesting to other colleagues or divisions in the company. Then, they **are pleased to help you along**."*

Palabras para recordar

to attend to: to take care of, to look after, to give one's attention to

without noticing: devoid of becoming aware, perceiving, detecting, or observing

to be divided into: to be split, separated, partitioned, or broken up into

by chance: by accident, coincidence, fortuity, or fate

division manager: head of a department, section, group, or branch

to draw the conclusion: to take the necessary steps

directions: courses, routes, paths, avenues

to introduce one to: to present one to, to familiarise or acquaint one with

to enjoy doing something: to take pleasure in, get pleasure from, or like doing something

to be pleased to help one along: to be happy, delighted, or glad to assist one

mediator: middleman, liaison, go-between, intermediary, third party

principal: most important, chief, main, most influential, leading

environment: surroundings, situation, background, circumstances

(continúa)

Continuación

---

to be responsible for: to be in charge of, accountable for, or liable for

---

impartial: unbiased, neutral, balanced, fair-minded, open-minded, objective

---

semi: half, partially, partly

Opening a new door to key accounts

There are various possibilities for *seeking out* key accounts. It is important, however, to accurately *judge* the *prospects for* a successful collaboration.

The "biggest" customer is not automatically the best customer. This experience was yet again made by key account manager Frank L. from Offenbach a couple of weeks ago, *"Comparing numbers and looking at the **bottom line** may **reveal** that the smaller business deals are surprisingly often more profitable than the bigger ones."*

Still, in many companies, key accounts are evaluated and selected according to their sales volume, *"**Erroneously**, a very **demanding** customer is regarded as more attractive, because you are proud to have won such a customer,"* says Frank L. *"The **low-maintenance** customers are often **underrated** in that regard."*

The key account manager, therefore, fundamentally *revamped* his acquisition strategy, *"A key account has **to be in line with** company policy: otherwise it is not worth the effort."*

A good quality key account equals a customer who, according to Frank L.:

✔ has few special requests and ***can be attended to easily*** with the existing range of products.

✔ has wishes that are representative of many more customers. *"It is worthwhile to head special pilot projects with them, because many other customers will follow their lead."*

✔ has problems which can be solved effortlessly and successfully within the existing range of services.

*"A key account relationship **has to be geared towards** a long-term partnership,"* says Frank L. *"A trusting and close collaboration is generally the key to the customer. Once he realises the advantages this collaboration brings him, he will willingly **commit himself to** our company long-term."*

Marry in haste, repent at leisure

Because the acquisition of and the care and support for a key account is very intensive, the following ***issues*** have to be resolved first. Only then can it be clearly seen to what extent it is actually worth going to win the key account:

✔ Which demands does the customer in fact have in regard to his supplier? This question can be clarified during an initial meeting with the help of a well thought-out ***questionnaire***, which the salesperson and the customer can ***peruse*** together.

✔ According to which criteria does the key account select his most important suppliers? Here, the customer has to explain his demands in a precise manner. If he is not prepared to do so or if it ***becomes obvious*** that his demands are excessive, this is not a good sign.

✔ Which benefits does the key customer expect in regard to new products or services? These benefits can vary from customer to customer and that is why it is necessary to identify them for every single customer respectively. Here it is important find out how your own strengths compare to those of the competition.

The relationship aspect has to work

*"With a key account, **above all**, the relationship aspect has to work,"* says Frank L. *"especially if the customer is high-maintenance, you have to get along well on a personal level. Otherwise, it just won't work."*

The relationship aspect is the doorway to the key account in the first place, according to the key account manager, *"Only when the climate is right and you like and respect each other, can the necessary trust develop."* That is precisely why Frank L. sets aside a lot of time for his key accounts, especially during the ***initial stage*** of his work, *"I have to know what kind of person my customer is, his likes and dislikes, what he prefers to do in his **spare time** and which atmosphere he feels most comfortable in."* A good source of information is always the assistant, *"She can even tell me which restaurant to choose for inviting my customer to lunch or dinner."*

Frank L. describes his strategy for ***"capturing"*** key accounts as follows:

- ✔ Define the criteria that a key account has to fulfill.

- ✔ Define the strengths and the benefits that your company can offer to the key account, respectively define the advantages of a long-term commitment.

- ✔ Find out, during the initial meetings, how the customer ***envisages*** an ideal partnership.

- ✔ Build solid ***interpersonal relationships***.

- ✔ Develop plans and strategies for a partnership together.

Palabras para recordar

key account: profitable, lucrative, moneymaking, major, or important customer

to seek out: to try to find, to hunt for, to pursue, to be after

to judge: to estimate, to assess, to guess, to surmise, to guesstimate

prospects for: likelihood or possibility of, chances for

bottom line: end result, outcome

to reveal: to show, to uncover, to bring to light

erroneously: incorrectly, wrongly, inaccurately, mistakenly, fallaciously

demanding: challenging, hard to please, insistent, taxing, difficult

low-maintenance: undemanding, easy to care for or get along with

underrated: undervalued, underestimated, not done justice to, rated too low

to revamp: to overhaul, to recondition, to fix up, to give a face-lift to

to be in line with: to be in accord, in step, in conformity, or in rapport with

can be attended to easily: can be taken care of, dealt with, or seen to without difficulty

has to be geared towards: has to be aimed or directed towards

to commit oneself to: to bind, dedicate, or obligate oneself to

marry in haste, repent at leisure: if you do something in a hurry, you may regret it for a long time

issues: points at issue, questions

questionnaire: opinion poll, survey

(continúa)

Continuación

to peruse: to read thoroughly or carefully, to examine, to scrutinise, to check

to become obvious: to come to be clear, noticeable, recognisable, or evident

above all: most of all, especially, in particular, primarily, principally

initial stage: start-up period, early stage, opening

spare time: leisure time, time off, free time

to capture: to win over, to secure, to gain, to catch, to grab hold of

to envisage something: to imagine, foresee, visualise, picture, see, or anticipate something

interpersonal relationships: human relations

Be proactive in getting referrals

Almost everyone in sales has heard *appreciative* words from their customers. But not enough salespeople ask for a written recommendation.

Positive feedback from customers is the best advertisement for sales representatives, their companies, and their products – *provided that* it is made public. Especially valuable are written testimonials created by people whose opinion *is highly esteemed* among a large circle of potential customers.

For management consultant Alexander Christiani from Starnberg it *is imperative* to document the *credible* statements of satisfied and enthusiastic customers. In his opinion, something in writing is much more convincing than the spoken word.

Take calculated steps

There is one problem: *Rarely* does a customer *feel bound to compose* a referral letter. Even if you ask him for it, you must *reckon with having to broach the subject again* until the whole matter *becomes embarrassing* to you.

 Christiani, therefore, recommends keeping matters firmly under control by offering to formulate the referral letter for the customer.

 Example: A customer just made some positive remarks about your products. You seize the opportunity and ask him to give you those remarks in writing, which the customer assures you he will do. You thank the customer and continue with the sales talk.

After a few minutes you return to the subject "referral" *emphasising* how pleased you are about the customer's promise. At the same time, suggest *to relieve him from the bulk of the work* by writing up *a draft* which the customer could modify if need be. According to the experience of Alexander Christiani, *"most customers gladly agree to this procedure. And if we **do the preliminary** work, eight out of ten customers feel obligated to keep their word and send the referral back."*

Palabras para recordar

referrals: recommendations, references

appreciative: approving, admiring, positive, enthusiastic

provided that: as long as, on the condition that, with the provision that

to be highly esteemed: to be greatly respected, regarded, or valued

to be imperative: to be very important, vital, crucial, or necessary

(continúa)

Continuación

credible: believable, convincing, realistic, trustworthy

to take calculated steps: to take deliberate, purposeful, or planned measures

rarely: hardly ever, seldom, not often

to feel bound: to feel compelled, obliged, or obligated

to compose: to write, to create, to make up, to think up, to formulate

to reckon with: to deal with, to handle, to contend with, to face

to have to broach the subject again: to have to bring up the issue another time

to become embarrassing: to become uncomfortable, discomforting, or awkward

to emphasise: to call attention to, to underscore, to underline

to relieve someone from something: to free, unburden, or liberate someone from something

the bulk of the work: the greater part, the main part, or the largest part of the task

a draft: an outline, a rough sketch

to do the preliminary work: to do the groundwork or first round

Is the ABC-analysis still up-to-date?

Using the *appropriate* controlling instruments helps you to focus on the "right" customers.

In the classical ABC analysis, customers are *ranked* on the basis of a certain *criterion*, mostly by sales volume, and separated into groups of important A customers and less important B and C customers.

Herein lies, in many cases, the critical *error* in the system because *merely* one criterion is *singled out* and examined. However, a customer's *well-established* evaluation cannot be based on one criterion alone.

Therefore, several strategically important parameters should be included in order *to arrive* at a *compelling* assessment of customers, for example:

✔ ***Contribution margin.***

✔ Competitive activities.

✔ ***Credit worthiness.***

✔ Terms of payment.

✔ Willingness to cooperate.

✔ Need for supervision.

✔ Position in the market.

✔ Innovative energy.

✔ Product mix policy.

✔ Marketing concept.

✔ Policy on pricing and conditions.

✔ Organisational structure.

If several criteria are applied for classifying the customers, this is called a multifactor analysis or a scoring model. Using a point rating system, the criteria are then brought into a ranking. In order *to detect* the difference in relevance *pertaining to* these criteria, they need to be evaluated *according to* their importance.

But these are not the only *tools* that are available to sales controlling. As an addition to the ABC analysis or the multifactor analysis, the following *approaches* are an option:

- ✔ Classification of customer status according to loyalty.
- ✔ Customer life cycle (CLC).
- ✔ Portfolio analysis.
- ✔ Customer lifetime value (CLV).
- ✔ Analysis of customer *approval.*

Palabras para recordar

appropriate: suitable, right, accurate, proper, fitting, apt

to rank: to position, to put in a specific order, to categorise, to classify

criterion: decisive factor, standard, measure, norm, benchmark, classic example

error: mistake, inaccuracy, miscalculation, flaw, fault, misconception

merely: only, just, purely, simply

to single out: to separate out, to set apart, to pick, to choose, to decide on

well-established: well-founded, well-grounded, well-substantiated

to arrive at: to come to, to reach, to attain, to make

compelling: conclusive, convincing, weighty, telling

contribution margin: profit contribution, variable gross profit, marginal income

credit worthiness: credit rating, credit status, financial standing

to detect: to discern, to make out, to spot, to distinguish, to identify

pertaining to: relating to, applying to, having a relevance to

(continúa)

Continuación

according to: in the order of, in agreement with,
in harmony with, in compliance with

tools: resources, instruments, aides

approach: method, procedure, technique, means, way

approval: satisfaction, contentment, endorsement

Vocabulario: inglés-español

. . . .

A

above all: sobre todo

accessibility: accesibilidad

accessories: accesorios

accomplishment: logro

according to: conforme a

achievement: logro, rendimiento

acquaintances: conocidos

actual: verdadera

acute awareness: atención profunda

addressed: abordó

adult education centre: centros de educación para adultos

advanced training: formación avanzada

affinity: afinidad

aforementioned: anteriormente mencionado

ahead: adelantar

allotted: asignado

ample: amplias

annoyance: fastidio

annual appraisals: evaluaciones anuales

anxious ones: preocupados

apparent: evidente

appreciative: de admiración, positivas

approach: enfoque, método

appropriate: adecuado

approval: satisfacción

are merging as: están fusionándose como

are regarded as: ser considerado como

are solicited: se solicitan

are supposed to: se supone que

as a given: como un dato objetivo

ascertained: asegurarse de

aside from: aparte de

assertive: asertivo, firme

assessment: evaluación, valoración

assumption: premisa

at an early stage: sin tardar

at the expense of: a expensas de

at the hazard: bajo riesgo de

attached to: unido a

attention: atención

attentively: atentamente, con atención

available: disponible

awkward: problemático

awkwardly: torpemente

B

back then: en aquella época

backing: respaldo

bear in mind: tener en cuenta

beforehand: de antemano

behaviour: comportamiento

believing: creyendo

belly: instintivo

beneficial: beneficioso

beyond that: aparte de eso

beyond: más allá

blows below the belt: golpes bajos

bottom line: balance final

boundary: límite

bouquet: ramo

branch: sucursal

brand: marca

brand perception: percepción de marca

breakdown: fallos

brief: breve

bulk of the work: la carga más pesada del trabajo

buyer's remorse: remordimiento del comprador

buzzword: palabra de moda

by chance: por casualidad

C

call for action: necesidad de actuar

call report: informe de visita

call: visita

calmly: con calma

calmness: calma

can be attended to easily: es posible atenderle fácilmente

can only be retained: solo se puede conservar

candy manufacturer: fabricante de confitería

cannot be maintained: no se puede mantener

capable: capaz

capital goods: bienes de equipo

challenging: desafiante

cheerfully: con satisfacción

choice: opción, elección

clashing: coincidencia

clear distinction: distinción clara

clearly defined boundary: una frontera claramente definida

closet: armario

clue: indicios, pista

clumsiness: torpeza

cold call: llamada en frío

collaboration: colaboración

collected: recopilada

combination lock: combinación de seguridad

comfort: consuelo

commercial vehicle: vehículo comercial

commitment: compromiso

committed: comprometido

comparable to: parecido a

comparatively rare: relativamente inusual

comparison: comparación

compelling: convincente

completion: conclusión

comprehensive: exhaustiva

comprehensively: exhaustivamente

concerns: preocupaciones

concession: concesión

conclusive: decisivo

condescending: condescendiente

conducted by: dirigido por, realizado por

confirmation: confirmación

conjoint: conjunto

connection with: conexión con

connection: conexión

consciously adopted: adoptado deliberadamente

consciously: deliberadamente, de forma deliberada

consciousness: conciencia

consequently: por consiguiente

considerably: considerablemente

consideration: reflexiones

consolidated scientific findings: hallazgos científicos contrastados

construction equipment: equipos de construcción

continually: continuamente

continuous: continuo

contributing to: que contribuye a

contribution margin: margen de beneficio

conveniences: comodidades

convincingly: convincentemente

core: esencia, núcleo

corner seating unit: rincón para sentarse

corporate citizenship: ciudadanía organizativa

corrective measure: medida correctora

correlating term: término relacionado

counterpart: la otra parte

cowardly: de forma cobarde

creation: creación

credible: verosímil

credit worthiness: calificación crediticia

criterion: criterio

crucial: crucial, esencial

current: actual, presente, vigente

customised: personalizado

custom-tailored: adaptado al cliente

D

decisive: decisivo, determinante

deficiency: deficiencia

delay: retrasos

delineation: delimitación

demeanour: comportamiento

dependability: formalidad

depreciated: menospreciado

desire: deseo

desired: deseada

despite: a pesar de

device: aparato

devoid of: carentes de

did the trick: fueron eficaces

directions: vías

disadvantage: desventaja

disapproval: desaprobación

discrepancy: discrepancias

distinction: distinción

distinctly: con precisión

division manager: director de división

doer: persona dinámica

donated to: donado a

doomed: desastre

doubts: dudas

downright: claramente

downside: inconveniente

draft: un borrador

drawing: dibujos

due to: como consecuencia de, debido a

E

easy-going: relajado

editorial department: departamento editorial

either way: de cualquier forma

elaborate: muy elaborados, compleja

elbow room: margen de maniobra

embarrassment: situaciones embarazosas

emphasising: enfática

encouraging: alentador

endurance: tenacidad

enlightening: revelador

ensuing: posterior, siguiente

entire: entero, completo

entrepreneurial: empresarial

environment: entorno

erroneously: erróneamente

error: error

esteemed: respetado

evaluation: evaluación

everything from one source: todo en un único proveedor

exception to the rule: excepción a la regla

expectations: expectativas

exploratory talk: charla de exploración

extended: prolongado

extension to the building: incorporación al edificio

extensive: amplias, fundamentales

exterior: exterior

extras: extras

F

faded: descolorido

failure: fracaso

fashion: manera, moda

fast pace: ritmo rápido

fear: temor

firm order of events: clara secuencia de acontecimientos

flexible work time: horario de trabajo flexible

flogged to death: utilizado hasta la saciedad

forces: fuerzas

foreman: capataz

foremost: más importante

frame: situación

free space: margen de movimiento

frequently: frecuentemente

friction: fricción

from rural areas: procedente de áreas rurales

fuel: combustible

furniture and fixtures: muebles e instalaciones

future: futuro

G

gateway: puerta

gaze: mirada

geared towards: orientada hacia

gender: género

generous: generoso

genuine: verdadera

gossip: chismorreos

grace period: periodo de gracia

gratuitously: gratis

guild: gremio

guilty party: la parte culpable

H

hardly any: casi ningún

harmful: perjudicial

has determined: ha llegado a la conclusión

has to be geared towards: debe estar dirigida a

hazardous: peligroso

head of engineering: jefe de ingeniería

high risk of failure: riesgo elevado de fallo

high-profile: impresionante

host: anfitrión

I

idiosyncrasy: idiosincracia, rareza

impartial: imparcial

imperative: imprescindible

implementation: implementación, puesta en práctica, aplicación

implications: repercusiones

in accordance with: de conformidad con, según

in advance: de antemano

in an instant: de inmediato

in compliance with: con observancia de

in favour of: a favor de

in particular: en concreto

in regard to: con respecto a, en relación con

in the preliminary stage: en la etapa preliminar

in vain: en vano

incidentally: a propósito

inciting: alentador

indeed: realmente

independent of: con independencia de

in-depth: exhaustivo

industrious: trabajador

inexpertly: con poca pericia

inhibition: reservas

inhibitions: inhibiciones

initial: inicial

initial stage: etapa inicial

initially: inicialmente

innocent victim: víctima inocente

insignificant: insignificante

instead of: en vez de

interest: intereses

interfering: molesto

interpersonal relationships: relaciones interpersonales

interposed questions: preguntas interpuestas

introductory: introductorio

involved: implicados

involvement: participación

issue: cuestión, asunto

it can be determined: se puede determinar

J

joint: conjunto

judgement: opinión

judging by your look: a juzgar por su mirada

K

key: clave, fundamental

key account: cuenta principal

knowledge for the sake of control: información para mantener el control

L

lack of: una falta de

lapse: fallo

largely: básicamente

lavish: complejas

lead: contacto, sugerencia

lecture: charla

leeway: margen

leisure time: tiempo de ocio

less obvious: menos evidente

link: conexión, vínculo

lively: animada

lone fighter: luchador solitario

long drawn-out: prolijo

loss: pérdida

low profit contribution: aportación baja al beneficio

low-maintenance: poco exigentes

M

mainly: principalmente

major: gran, importante

making something reach its peak: conseguir que algo llegue a su punto máximo

marry in haste, repent at leisure: antes de casarte, mira lo que haces

mastermind: cerebro

matching: complementario, combinar, correspondiente

matter: cuestión, materia

matter-of-factly: de forma clara

measure: medida

mechanical engineering company: empresa de ingeniería mecánica

mediator: mediador

merely: meramente

mindset: modo de pensar

minor detail: detalle insignificante, detalle mínimo

minor: insignificante

miserly: austero

mistake: error

mistaken for: confundido con

mood: humor

more probing: más detallado

most promising: el más prometedora

mountaineer: alpinista

much greater challenge: reto más difícil

multifaceted: variado, polifacético

mumbling: murmurar

N

negotiation: negociación

nevertheless: no obstante

new guy: el recién llegado

nonchalantly: con aire despreocupado

not to mention: por no mencionar

O

objection: objeciones

objective: objetivo

obliged: obligado

obstacle: obstáculo

obvious: evidente, obvias

obviously: obviamente

occupation: trabajo

of all concerned: de todos los afectados

of one's own accord: por su cuenta

on average: por lo general

on behalf of: en nombre de

on difficult terrain: en campos difíciles

on what terms they are with someone: cómo se llevan con alguien

one is dealt a blow: uno sufre un revés

one-of-a-kind: inigualable

opinion-forming: creador de opinión

order of precedence: orden de prioridad

outdated: desfasado

outside observer: observador externo

outside supplier: proveedor externo

overall sales: ventas generales

overheard: oír casualmente

owner: propietario

ownership: control

P

palm of one's hand: la palma de la mano

paper: documentos

paragraph: párrafo

particular: específico

particularities: singularidades

past: pasado

path: vía

peak performance: rendimiento máximo

perseverance: perseverancia

persuasive: convincente

pertaining to: referente a, relativa a

physical discomfort: malestar físico

pitfall: dificultad

pleasant: agradable

pleasantly: amablemente

pollution: contaminación

possibly: posiblemente

praise: elogios

preconceived: preconcebida

predecessor: predecesor

predetermined duration: duración preestablecida

predetermined: predeterminadas

prediction: predicción

prejudice: prejuicio

premise: premisa

premises: instalaciones

prerequisite: requisito indispensable, requisito previo

presence: presencia

present: existente

previous: anterior

previously: anteriormente

primarily: principalmente

principal: principal

probability: probabilidad

probing: indagatoria

process: proceso

processing speed: velocidad de funcionamiento

promising: prometedor

promptness: rapidez

prospective customer: cliente potencial

prospects for: posibilidades para

prospects: perspectivas

provided that: siempre que

provided: siempre que

provider: proveedor

psychological strain: presión, tensión psicológica

public figure: personaje público

purely: puramente

purpose: finalidades

purposefully: con determinación

pushy: agresivo

Q

quarrel: disputas

questionnaire: cuestionario

quirk: peculiaridad

quoted: mencionado

R

range: gama

rapport: relación de comunicación

rarely: raramente

rather: más bien

ready cash: dinero en metálico

really self-evident things: las cosas verdaderamente obvias

reasoning: razonamiento

recent: reciente

recently: recientemente

recipe: receta

reckoning: opinión

recognised: reconocido

recurring: recurrente

referral: referencia, recomendación

regardless: pase lo que pase

related: relacionado

related to: relacionado con

relating to: relacionado con

reliable: fiable

remarkable: extraordinario

remuneration: retribución

repeated: reiterado

repeatedly: reiteradamente

replacement purchases: compras de sustitución

replacement: sustituto

research establishment: organismo de investigación

resentment: resentimiento

resolved: resueltas

respective: respectivo

responsibility: responsabilidad

retention: conservación

revaluated: más importante

revealing: reveladora

revelation: revelación

revenue: ingresos

rewarded properly: recompensado de la forma adecuada

room for improvement: margen de mejora

S

sadly: lamentablemente

sales approach: enfoque, método de venta

sales pitch: discurso de venta

sample: muestra

scheduling of appointments: concertación de citas

security need: necesidad de seguridad

seemingly: aparentemente

selection: selección

self-actualisation: autorrealización

semi: semi

sensible: prudente

sensitive: delicado

set of tools: conjunto de herramientas

several: varias

shared: compartidas

shipping agency: agencia de transporte

sign of wear: indicio de deterioro

similar: parecida

sincere: sincero

single-mindedly: con determinación

site: planta

skilfully: con habilidad

skilled: experto

skills: habilidades

smoothly: con fluidez

so what: y qué

something to envision: imaginar algo

sophisticated: complicado

sound: sólido, consistente

source: fuente

spare part: pieza de repuesto

spare parts wholesaler: empresa mayorista de piezas de repuesto

spare time: tiempo libre

stable: estable

stall: pretexto

standing: posición

state-of-the-art: moderno, vanguardista

steady: habituales

stopgap: recurso provisional, último recurso

straight: sin parar

stroke of luck: golpe de suerte

structurally completed home: casa con las estructuras terminadas

stuff that dreams are made of: la materia de la que están hechos los sueños

subsequent: posterior

substantial: considerable

substantiated: justificado

subtle distinction: una sutil distinción

suffer from it: sufrir las consecuencias de

sufficient: suficiente

suitable: adecuada

superior objectives: objetivos superiores

supposed reason: causa supuesta

supposedly: supuestamente

surfacing: emergentes

surroundings: entorno

T

tailored to: adaptado a las necesidades de

tailor-made: personalizado

tangible: tangible

tardily: con retraso

task: tarea

tension: tensión

territory: área

that need to be taken into account: eso hay que tenerlo en cuenta

there is no clear-cut dividing line: no existe una línea divisoria claramente definida

this entails: esto entraña

thoughtless: irreflexivo

to a bare minimum: a lo justo

to abide by: atenerse a

to accelerate: acelerar

to accompany: acompañar

to accomplish: conseguir

to achieve: conseguir

to acknowledge: reconocer

to act as: desempeñar las funciones de

to act: actuar

to adapt: adaptar

to adapt to: adaptarse a

to adhere to: adherirse a, atenerse a, cumplir

to adjust: ajustar

to admit: admitir

to advise: aconsejar

to affect: afectar a

to affirm: ratificar

to aid: ayudar

to aim: aspirar

to alert someone to something: alertar a alguien sobre algo

to align something with something: ajustar algo a algo

to align: coordinar

to allege: alegar

to allot: repartir

to always move on the surface: ser superficial

to amplify: fortalecer

to appeal to someone: atraer a alguien

to appear aloof: parecer distante

to appear credible: ser verosímil

to apply especially to: ser de aplicación especialmente

to apply: aplicar

to appreciate: apreciar, valorar

to approach: abordar, dirigirse a, plantear

to arrive at: llegar a

to assemble: reunir

to assert: reafirmarse, aseverar

to assess: evaluar

to assign: asignar

to assume: dar por supuesto, adoptar, presuponer

to assure: asegurar

to attach great importance: atribuir gran importancia

to attain: conseguir

to attend: asistir

to attend to: atender a, ocuparse de

to attest: avalar

to attract attention: atraer la atención

to avoid: evitar

to awaken: despertar

to back something: respaldar algo

to bad-mouth someone: hablar mal de alguien

to bad-mouth something: denostar

to be a giveaway: delatar

to be a match for someone: estar a la altura de alguien

to be able to access: poder acceder

to be affected by something: estar afectado por algo

to be an integral part: ser parte integrante

to be annoyed: sentirse enojado

to be applied: aplicarse, ser de aplicación

to be assigned specifically: ser asignado específicamente

to be assigned to someone: estar asignado a alguien

to be at a loss: estar perplejo, no saber cómo reaccionar

to be attended to: estar atendidos

to be avoided at all costs: ser evitado a toda costa

to be aware of the fact: ser consciente del hecho

to be banished: ser borrado

to be banned from: ser eliminado de

to be called to account for something: ser obligado a responder de algo

to be common practise: ser práctica habitual

to be comparable to: ser comparable a

to be compiled: ser recopilado

to be comprised of: estar compuesta de

to be confused with: confundir con

to be convinced: estar convencido

to be covered against something: estar cubierto frente a algo

to be crucial: ser crucial

to be cut down: quedar limitado

to be divided into: estar dividido en

to be easily cajoled: ser engatusado fácilmente

to be engaged in: estar implicado en

to be entitled to something: tener derecho a algo

to be equipped with: estar equipado con

to be especially on guard: estar especialmente alerta

to be exhausted soon: agotarse pronto

to be extremely sensitive: ser extremadamente sensible

to be fine and dandy: estar perfecto

to be fixated on someone: tener fijación con alguien

to be flabbergasted: quedarse pasmado

to be forced on someone: imponerse a alguien

to be fully justified by: estar plenamente justificado por

to be furnished with: estar amueblada con

to be geared towards: estar pensado con el propósito de

to be highly esteemed: tener en alta estima

to be imperative: ser esencial

to be in a hurry: tener prisa

to be in charge of: estar a cargo de

to be in for a surprise: llevarse una sorpresa

to be in line with: seguir la línea de

to be in vain: ser en vano

to be incorporated: incluirse

to be indispensable: ser indispensable

to be key: ser esencial

to be lacking: carecer

to be much more favourable to be much better, to be much more beneficial: ser mucho más favorable, ser más beneficioso

to be naturally imbedded in something: estar integrado con naturalidad

to be not more inclined to do something: no sentirse más inclinado a hacer algo

to be nurtured: ser alimentado

to be outsourced: ser subcontratado

to be part of something: formar parte de algo

to be perceived as trustworthy: considerar que se es digno de confianza

to be pleased to help one along: estar encantado de ayudar a alguien

to be pressed for time: tener poco tiempo

to be proud of something: estar orgulloso de algo

to be put to the test: ser puesto a prueba

to be resolved: ser resuelto

to be responsible for: ser responsable de

to be responsive to something: ser receptivo ante algo

to be rounded: estar terminado

to be suitable: encajar

to be suited alike: ser igualmente indicado

to be suited for something: ser adecuado, apropiado para algo

to be tailored to: estar adaptado

to be taken into account: ser tenido en cuenta

to be taken under someone's wing: ser tomado bajo la protección de alguien

to be the most promising: ser el más prometedor

to be thrilled: estar encantado

to be too focused on someone: centrarse excesivamente en alguien

to be tremendously accommodating: ser extremadamente flexible

to be truly convinced of something: estar verdaderamente convencido de algo

to be very much in tune with something: estar perfectamente coordinado con algo

to be worried: estar preocupado

to bear cost-effectiveness in mind: tener en cuenta la relación coste-eficiencia

to beat about the bush: andarse con rodeos

to become aware of: tomar conciencia de

to become embarrassing: sentirse apurado

to become obvious: hacerse patente

to become obvious: quedar claro

to blame: culpar

to bond: adherir, establecer, afianzar

to boost: mejorar

to bother: molestar

to brief: informar

to bring in line: coordinar

to bring something into play: sacar algo a colación

to broach: plantear

to build up tension: crear tensión

to call it a day: terminar la jornada

to call on: solicitar

to capture: conseguir

to carry out: realizar

to catch: encontrarse

to cause one a lot of grievance: causar muchos quebraderos de cabeza

to cause one considerable anguish: causar a alguien sufrimiento

to check out: comprobar

to choose: decidir

to claim: alegar

to cling to: atenerse a

to coerce: coaccionar

to come across as: dar la impresión de

to come out of one's shell: salir del cascarón

to commence: comenzar

to commit: comprometer

to commit oneself to: comprometerse

to complement: complementar

to compose: elaborar, redactar

to comprise: abarcar, componer

to conceal: ocultar

to conduct: llevar a cabo

to confer: consultar

to confer obligingly: consultar amablemente con

to congratulate someone: dar la enhorabuena a alguien

to consider: plantearse, tener en cuenta

to consist of: estar compuesto de, consistir en

to constitute: constituir

to contain oneself: contenerse

to contemplate: plantearse

to contribute: contribuir

to contribute one's share: poner de su parte

to convey: comunicar, transmitir

to convince: convencer

to corner one: arrinconar a alguien

to count more than: ser más importante que

to count on: confiar en

to cover up: ocultar

to crop up: ocurrir

to curtail: reducir

to dawdle: malgastar el tiempo

to dawn on one: venir a la cabeza

to decline: declinar, disminuir, rechazar

to decline without further explanation: decir que no sin más explicación

to deepen: profundizar

to delve into: analizar

to demand: exigir, requerir

to depend on someone: depender de alguien

to depend on: depender de

to depend upon: depender de

to derive: obtener

to derive from: derivarse de, conseguir de

to deserve: merecer

to deserve equal treatment: merecer igual trato

to desire: desear

to destroy: destruir

to detect: detectar

to determine: determinar, averiguar

to differentiate: diferenciar

to diminish: suavizar

to discern: distinguir

to discover: descubrir

to dismantle something: desmantelar algo

to display: mostrar

to disprove: rebatir

to distract: distraer

to divert from something: desviar de algo

to do one's share: hacer la parte que le corresponde a uno

to do the preliminary work: hacer el trabajo preliminar

to drag out: posponer, prolongar

to draw a conclusion: extraer una conclusión

to draw the conclusion: llegar a la conclusión

to draw up: elaborar

to drift into triteness: caer en la trivialidad

to drop some appropriate cues: dejar caer claves adecuadas

to ease: aliviar, facilitar

to elapse: transcurrir

to elongate: alargar

to embellish: adornar

to emerge: surgir

to emphasise: hacer hincapié, recalcar

to encounter: tropezar, encontrarse

to encounter rejection: encontrar rechazo

to encourage: animar

to endeavour on: esforzarse por

to endure: soportar

to enjoy doing something: disfrutar haciendo algo

to enjoy their effect to the fullest: disfrutar al máximo de los efectos

to enrol: inscribirse

to ensue: tener lugar a continuación, producirse

to ensure: asegurarse

to entail: entrañar

to enter: introducir

to envisage something: concebir algo

to envision: imaginar

to envision in one's mind: visualizar en la mente de uno mismo

to escort repair shop: taller de reparaciones

to exceed: superar

to exchange: intercambiar

to exclude: excluir

to experience: experimentar

to explore: sondear

to express: expresar

to exude: irradiar, mostrar

to face someone: hacer frente a alguien

to facilitate: facilitar

to fail: no (hacer algo)

to fall through: no concretarse, quedar en nada

to feature: ofrecer, presentar

to feel angry toward: sentirse enojado con

to feel bound: sentirse obligado

to feel flattered: sentirse halagado

to feel very strongly about something: ser muy apasionado de algo

to figure out: averiguar

to find it inappropriate: considerar que es inapropiado

to fizzle out: apagarse

to force down: presionar a la baja

to force something down: conseguir que algo descienda

to foresee: prever

to fret about something: preocuparse de

to function without a hitch: funcionar sin fallos

to gain: conseguir, ganar, adquirir, lograr

to gather: recopilar

to get accustomed to: habituarse a

to get into: pasar a

to get one's way: salirse con la suya

to get rid of someone: deshacerse de alguien

to get something off the ground: hacer que algo despegue

to get the subject across: transmitir el mensaje

to give in to: caer en la tentación

to give one that edge: colocar a alguien en posición de ventaja

to give oneself away: delatarse

to give proof: proporcionar pruebas

to go haywire: ir mal

to go off without a hitch: discurrir sin problemas

to go to great trouble over something: tener muchos problemas con algo

to guide someone through something: orientar a alguien a través de algo

to haggle the price down: negociar a la baja el precio

to happen to be away on holiday: estar de vacaciones

to happen to be fortunate: tener suerte con

to have a hotline to heaven: tener poderes paranormales

to have an edge on someone: tener una ventaja sobre alguien

to have an impact on something: tener repercusión sobre algo

to have been a long time coming: forjarse a lo largo del tiempo

to have fully adjusted to something: haberse adaptado completamente a algo

to have gotten into the habit of doing something: coger la costumbre de hacer algo

to have harmful effects on something: tener efectos perjudiciales sobre algo

to have in common with someone: tener en común con alguien

to have something reconfirmed: reconfirmar algo

to have succeeded: haber tenido éxito

to have to acquaint oneself intensely with: tener que familiarizarse con

to have to be quoted: tener que ser citado

to have to broach the subject again: volver a plantear la cuestión

to have trust in someone: tener confianza en alguien

to highlight: resaltar

to impair: dañar

to implement: poner en práctica, implantar

to imply: entrañar

to impress upon someone: inculcar

to impress: impresionar

to increase: aumentar

to indicate: indicar

to interlink: interconectar

to introduce one to: presentarse a

to invoke: invocar

to join in: unirse a

to judge: valorar, juzgar

to jump to: pasar directamente a

to keep one's composure: mantener su compostura

to keep someone on tenterhooks intentionally: tener a alguien sobre ascuas deliberadamente

to keep something alive: mantener algo vivo

to keep something available: hacer disponible

to keep track of something: llevar un seguimiento de algo

to keep up: mantenerse

to land off the mark: acabar equivocándose

to lastingly secure: asegurar de forma duradera

to leave: abandona

to limit oneself to: limitarse a

to liven up: animar

to long for something: anhelar algo

to look into: analizar

to mainly affect: afectar principalmente a

to maintain: mantener, conservar

to make a cut: hacer un «corte»

to make flimsy excuses: poner excusas baladíes

to make it a habit: adquirir la costumbre

to make something accessible to someone: conseguir que algo sea asequible para alguien

to make the difference: marca la diferencia

to mark: marcar

to master the art of something: dominar el arte de hacer algo

to matter: importar

to measure: medir

to meet: satisfacer

to memorise the fine print to remember or learn by heart the small lettering: memorizar la letra pequeña, recordar la letra pequeña

to mention: mencionar

to monitor: vigilar

to move forward with someone: avanzar con alguien

to neglect: descuidar

to not arise: no producirse

to not be able to complain about: no poder quejarse sobre

to not be trustworthy: no ser digno de confianza

to not beat about the bush: no andarse por las ramas

to not leave it at: no pararse en

to not materialise: no materializarse

to not proceed according to plan: no discurrir según lo previsto

to not regard: no considerar

to not slip into: no derivar

to nourish: alentar

to nudge someone onto something: incitar a alguien a algo

to nurture: desarrollar

to obtain: conseguir

to occur: suceder

to offer benefit: ofrecer ventajas

to offer compensation: ofrecer compensación por

to outshine: superar

to overrate: sobrevalorar

to oversee: supervisar

to own: ser el propietario de

to paint a clear picture of something: describir claramente

to paint a vivid picture of something: plasmar una imagen clara de algo

to pass on: transmitir a, trasladar

to pay dearly for something: pagar caro algo

to pay off: merecer la pena

to pay the same degree of attention to each prospect: prestar el mismo grado de atención a cada cliente potencial

to pay: merecer la pena

to perceive: percibir, considerar

to persuade someone to do something: convencer a alguien de algo

to peruse: leer detenidamente

to pick up the thread: retomar el hilo

to place ads: poner anuncios

to play it safe: apostar sobre seguro

to play out: acabar

to pleasantly surprise someone: sorprender gratamente a alguien

to pocket: embolsarse

to pool: agrupar

to possess: poseer

to postpone: posponer

to prefer: preferir

to pretend not to be there: fingir que no está allí

to prevail: existir

to prevent something: impedir algo

to prevent: impedir

to probe deeper into something: indagar más detenidamente

to proceed: proceder

to progress: progresar

to prompt: inducir a, motivar, provocar

to prospect: buscar clientes nuevos

to prove: demostrar

to prove someone right: dar la razón a alguien

to provide: proporcionar

to provoke: provocar

to provoke protest: provocar protestas

to push for cost-saving measures: promover medidas de ahorro de costes

to push someone to do something: empujar a alguien a hacer algo

to put discussion of price on the backburner: dejar en segundo plano la discusión sobre el precio

to put one's foot in one's mouth: meter la pata

to put pressure on someone: presionar a

to put someone under pressure: presionar a alguien

to put the screws to someone: apretarle los tornillos a alguien

to question one's assumption: cuestionar la propia suposición

to quote: citar, indicar

to raise: elevar, mejorar

to raise awareness: mejorar la conciencia

to raise someone's anticipation: aumentar las ilusiones de alguien

to rank: clasificar

to rank among: estar englobado en un grupo

to reap: recoger

to reassess: replantearse

to reassure someone: tranquilizar a alguien

to recharge: recargar

to reckon: considerar

to reckon with: enfrentarse a

to recognise: identificar, reconocer

to reconsider: replantearse

to re-examine: reconsiderar

to refer to: hacer referencia a

to refute: refutar

to regard: considerar

to regret: antiguo

to reinforce: reforzar

to release: dejar disponible

to rely on: recurrir a

to remain in charge of: seguir a cargo de

to remain matter-of-fact: mantener la objetividad

to remain unfazed: mantenerse imperturbable

to remain: mantener, permanecer

to reply: responder

to require: requerir

to resolve the issue: resolver la cuestión

to resort to: recurrir a

to respond: responder

to respond to: responder a

to respond to something: responder a algo

to restrain oneself: contenerse, retraerse

to retain: retener, conservar

to revamp: reformar

to reveal: revelar

to review: revisar

to revise: revisar

to rid someone of something: librar a alguien de algo

to rouse: despertar

to run the gauntlet: pasar revista

to scare: amedrentar

to schedule an appointment: programar una cita

to score with someone: causar una gran impresión

to scrutinise: examinar

to secure: asegurarse, garantizar

to see to it: encargarse de

to seek out: buscar

to seize: aprovechar, calibrar

to sense: tener la sensación

to serve as: servir de

to serve as an extension of something: funcionar como una extensión de algo

to set a precedent: fijar un precedente

to set one's sights on: tener la mira puesta en

to set up: organizar, conseguir, crear

to set up appointments: concertar citas

to settle into one's new job: adaptarse al nuevo trabajo

to share: compartir

to single out: escoger

to snub: desairar

to sound out: sondear

to speed up: agilizar

to spoil: estropear

to squint: entrecerrar los ojos

to steer: dirigir

to strengthen: reforzar

to struggle with something: tener problemas para hacer algo

to subdivide: subdividir

to submit: presentar

to suffer: resentirse, sufrir

to suffice: ser suficiente, bastar

to supervise: supervisar

to surround: rodear

to sustain: mantener

to sweat the small stuff: preocuparse por los pequeños detalles

to tackle: abordar

to take action: adoptar medidas

to take advantage of something: sacar provecho de algo

to take apart: desglosar

to take calculated steps: dar pasos calculados

to take into considera-tion: tener algo en cuenta, tener en consideración

to take precedence: tener prioridad

to take someone to task: reprender a alguien

to take something se-riously: tomarse algo en serio

to tempt: tentar

to tense up: ponerse tenso

to throw in the towel: tirar la toalla

to throw someone off: coger a alguien por sorpresa

to tie someone to so-mething: vincular a alguien con algo

to tie someone to: vincular a alguien

to tip the scales: inclinar la balanza a favor de alguien

to totter: tambalearse

to treat: tratar

to treat oneself to something: darse un capricho

to trigger: desencadenar

to trust: confiar

to turn special attention to: prestar especial atención a

to underline: subrayar

to utilise: utilizar

to view: considerar

to vindicate oneself: justificarse

to voice: expresar

to weigh every word: sopesar cada palabra

to what extent: en qué medida, hasta qué punto

to win over: ganarse

to withdraw: retirar

to witness: presenciar

to woo someone: cortejar a alguien

to yearn for: desear algo

toll-free: gratuito

tools: herramientas

topics: temas

touchstone: piedra de toque

trace: ápice

transition: transición

transition to: transición a

trap: trampa

trickiest: más espinosas

trusted: de confianza

trusting: de confianza

turning point: punto de inflexión

turnover: facturación

two-digit: dos dígitos

U

ultimately: al final

under the direction of: bajo la dirección de

underrated: minusvalorados

unflappable: imperturbable

unintentionally: de manera no deliberada

unnoticed: desapercibido

unsatisfactory: insatisfactorio

unserviceable: inservible

unspoken: tácito

upbeat fashion: manera optimista

uppermost: fundamental, principal

upset: enojado

urgency: urgencia

utility costs: costes de suministros o servicios

utilization: utilización

V

vain: vanidoso

valued: valorado

varied: diverso

variety of couplings: un surtido de conexiones

various: diversos

vehicle owner: propietario de vehículo

vicinity: proximidades

virtually: prácticamente

vital: esencial

vivid: gráfica

vividly: gráficamente

W

wage: salario

walk on a tightrope: peligroso

waste disposal: eliminación de residuos

wasted: perdido

way out: escapatoria

weaker: el más débil

well-established: bien fundamentado

well-meaning: bienintencionado

what became of something: cuál ha sido el resultado de algo

what is at your disposal: lo que está a su disposición

when in doubt: en caso de duda

which are in need of explanation: que necesita explicación

which can be accessed: que sea accesible

with regard to: con respecto a

within the realm: dentro del ámbito

without delay: sin demora

without noticing: sin
   darse cuenta

worrier: hipocondríaco

worry: preocupación

wrongdoing: mala acción

Y

yield: rendimiento

Glosario*

• • • • • • • • • • • • • • • • • • •

above all: most of all, especially, in particular, primarily, principally → 23, 58-59, 151, 153

accessibility: approachability, availability → 117-118

accessories: attachments, extras, add-ons, parts fixtures → 50, 52, 64

accomplishment: talent, skill, gift, achievement, performance, capability → 14, 34, 39, 127

according to: in keeping with, in accordance with, in agreement with, in line with, following, in conformity with, in the order of, in harmony with, in compliance with → 15, 21, 24, 26, 76, 83-84, 94-95, 120, 144, 148-151, 154, 156-158

achievement: accomplishment, capability, performance, activity, operation, running, working, success, accomplishment, feat → 14, 33-34, 39, 54, 56, 69, 127

acquaintances: associates, connections, contacts → 140-141

actual: real, concrete, factual, authentic, genuine → 6, 9-10, 39, 72, 91, 102, 131

acute awareness: keen alertness, attentiveness, responsiveness, or consciousness → 16-18

addressed: spoke of, talked about, described, communicated → 88, 90, 142

adult education centre: school or educational institution for grown-ups → 89

advanced training: further schooling → 64, 66

advice: counsel, guidance, opinion → 84, 88, 125, 127

affinity: partiality, attraction, liking, inclination → 117

aforementioned: previously described, abovementioned, forenamed, aforesaid → 144-146

---

* Los números remiten a las páginas de los párrafos que contienen la palabra indicada.

ahead: forward, to the front → 26, 40, 42, 49, 72, 74, 100, 145

allotted: designated, chosen, selected, assigned → 49, 51

ample: plenty of, more than enough, enough and to spare → 12, 14

annoyance: irritation, exasperation, frustration, aggravation, anger → 16, 18

annual appraisals: yearly assessments, evaluations, reviews, negotiations, or talks → 47-48

anxious ones: worried, concerned, fearful, apprehensive, uneasy, or nervous ones → 112, 114

apparent: obvious, clear, evident, plain, discernible → 47, 82, 108

appreciative: approving, admiring, positive, enthusiastic grateful, thankful, supportive, encouraging→ 12, 14, 105, 153-154

approach: method, procedure, modus operandi, technique, means, way, style, manner → 16, 49, 51, 75-76, 78, 104, 158

appropriate: proper, apt, suitable, correct, right, fitting, opportune, pertinent, accurate → 6-7, 33, 44, 59, 86-87, 97, 100, 132, 155, 157

approval: satisfaction, contentment, endorsement → 14, 157-158

as a given: as a matter-of-factness, as a matter-of-course → 27-28

ascertained: ensured, made sure → 82

aside from: apart from, notwithstanding, besides, except for, with the exception of, in addition to, on top of, besides → 27, 32, 64, 69, 77-78, 80-81, 133

assertive: forceful, aggressive, dynamic, self-assured, self-confident, forward, firm, bold → 33, 35, 64, 66

assessment: appraisal, evaluation, rating, estimation, judgement, review, gauging → 58-59, 79, 81, 120, 156

assumption: supposition, premise, belief, conjecture → 16, 18

at an early stage: promptly, without delay, early on, ahead of schedule → 143, 145

at the expense of: on account of, at the cost of, at the sacrifice of → 32, 34

at the hazard: at the risk, peril, or threat → 37, 39

attached to: fixed to, fastened to, stuck to, affixed to → 68, 77-78, 102

attention: awareness, consideration, notice, regard, recognition, heed → 8, 15, 17, 19, 23, 64, 67, 69, 73, 78-79, 81, 87, 89-90, 108, 121, 132, 136, 148, 155

attentively: carefully, alertly, conscientiously → 15, 17, 74-75

authority: expert, specialist, professional → 33, 97, 100

available: obtainable, accessible, existing → 22, 46, 70, 77, 79-81, 94, 156

awkward: problematic, tricky, difficult, complex → 6-7, 24, 155

awkwardly: clumsily, inelegantly, gracelessly, amateurishly → 11, 13

back then: in those early days, in those former times → 125, 127

backing: support, help, assistance, encouragement, cooperation → 44

beforehand: earlier, in advance, ahead of time, already, before now → 72, 74, 84, 97, 100

behaviour: actions, manners, ways, activities, conduct → 12, 21-22, 26, 28, 35, 37, 93, 112

believing: thinking, supposing, being of the opinion, assuming → 131-132

belly: instinctive, innate, gut → 23, 25

beneficial: conducive, agreeable, helpful → 20, 33, 35, 109, 130

beyond: outside the reach or limitations of, surpassing → 36, 43, 45, 86

beyond that: above that, in addition to that, outside of that, over and above that → 43, 45

blows below the belt: letdowns, setbacks, failures → 114-116

bottom line: end result, outcome → 149, 152

capital goods: investment or industrial commodities → 111, 113

challenge: test, trial → 18, 35, 43, 45, 99, 101

cheerfully: happily, joyfully, optimistically → 41-42

choice: option, alternative, possibility, solution, answer, way out, pick → 8-9, 133-134

clashing: conflict, coincidence, concurrence → 49, 51

clear distinction: explicit dividing line, separation, or differentiation → 118, 120

clearly defined boundary: plainly marked out, established, or settled demarcation line → 118, 120

closet: cabinet, cupboard → 114

clue: information, sign, hint, evidence, pointer, indication → 60

clumsiness: awkwardness, ungainliness, ineptness, gaucheness → 11, 13

cold call: unannounced visit at a prospective customer's company → 94, 96

collaboration: partnership, alliance, association, teamwork, group effort, cooperation → 32, 34, 43-44, 49, 51, 119, 149-150

collected: gathered, brought together, pulled together, accumulated → 35, 80-81, 128

combination lock: security device, safety feature → 27, 29

comfort: consolation, reassurance, relief, solace, help → 25, 144-145

commercial vehicle: utility van, bus, or lorry → 64, 66

commitment: attachment, allegiance → 37, 78, 99, 151

committed: dedicated, loyal, devoted, very involved → 98, 100

comparable to: like, similar to, akin to → 20-21, 109, 125, 127

comparatively rare: relatively infrequent, few and far between, or uncommon → 95-96

comparison: contrast, differentiation, collation, judgement, evaluation → 76

compelling: conclusive, convincing, weighty, telling, powerful → 69, 156-157

competitive: combative, competition oriented, ready for action → 65, 67, 119, 156

competitive advantage: having an edge over the rival or opponent → 65, 67

complaint: criticism, grievance, statement of dissatisfaction → 120

completion: close, conclusion, finish, ending, finalisation → 44, 46, 69, 103

comprehensive: all-inclusive, all-embracing, wide-ranging, exhaustive → 52, 101, 127

comprehensively: completely, thoroughly, exhaustively, in detail, carefully → 79, 81

concerns: apprehensions, trepidations, worries, fear, unease, disquiet → 84, 97, 100, 133, 135

concession: yielding, surrender, adjustment, modification, compromise → 35

condescending: patronising, snobbish → 124, 127

conducted by: carried out by, done by, performed by, organised or managed by → 50, 52, 64, 66, 76, 78

conjoint: shared, combined, concerted → 47-48

connection: link, association, bond → 38, 46, 58, 80-81, 123-124

connection with: link to, association with, relationship with, correlation to → 80-81

consciously: knowingly, wilfully → 17, 19

consciously adopted: deliberately, intentionally, wilfully, or knowingly assumed → 17, 19

consciousness: mind, thoughts, awareness, memory, cognizance → 18

consequently: as a result, so, therefore, hence, subsequently → 133

considerable: a great deal of, much, a lot of, a fair amount of, substantial, extensive, great, noticeable, significant → 53, 55, 111, 113

consideration: thought, deliberation, contemplation, reflection → 40, 42, 60, 67, 81, 92-93, 97, 99-100

consist of: involve, be made up of, include, embody, incorporate → 38, 56, 68, 104

consolidated scientific findings: confirmed results relating to the principles of science → 86, 89

constant, permanent conducted by: carried out, performed, run, organised, or handled by → 52

construction equipment: building tools or gear → 140-141

continually: repeatedly, frequently, regularly, constantly → 50, 71

continuous: non-stop, constant, perpetual, uninterrupted, incessant, → 43-44, 46, 50-52

contributing to: being instrumental or having a hand in achieving → 64, 66, 76

contribution margin: profit contribution, variable gross profit, marginal income → 121, 156-157

conveniences: comfort, amenities → 23, 25

convincingly: persuasively, credibly, believably, compellingly → 126-128

core: centre, central part, heart, essence, quintessence, nitty-gritty, focal point, foundation, basis, marrow → 36, 70-71, 74

corner seating unit: sitting area, lounge suite, settee arrangement, three-piece suite → 112, 114

corporate citizenship: social and cultural involvement (of businesses) → 77

corrective measure: remedial or counteractive course of action → 79, 81, 128-129

correlating term: corresponding, related, or associated phrase → 38

cowardly: gutlessly, spinelessly, weakly, lily-liveredly → 91, 93

creation: formation, making, establishment, construction → 27

credible: believable, convincing, realistic, trustworthy → 132, 134, 153-155

credit worthiness: credit rating, credit status, financial standing → 156-157

distinction: difference, dissimilarity, division, contrast → 16-18, 118, 120-121

distinctly: precisely, plainly → 94, 96

division manager: head of a department, section, group, or branch → 148

doer: go-getter, achiever, organiser, active person → 60

donated to: given to, contributed to, bestowed upon, provided for → 77-78

doubts: a lack of confidence or faith, uneasiness, apprehension, misgivings, qualms, uncertainties, worries, fears, suspicions → 94, 97, 100

downright: blatantly, utterly, completely, totally, absolutely, out-and-out → 124, 126-127

downside: disadvantage, danger, negative consequence, harm, drawback, difficulty, snag, snare → 95

draft: outline, rough sketch → 154-155

due to: because of, attributable to, because of, by reason of, on account of, owing to, as a result of, caused by → 54, 56, 134-135

easy-going: relaxed, laidback, informal, casual → 8-9

editorial department: section of a publishing house where newspaper content is written up → 90

effort: attempt, endeavour, try → 34, 82, 100-101, 131, 146, 149

either: both, each → 16, 108, 144

either way: one way or another, whichever way you look at it, somehow or other → 108

elaborate: complex, detailed, involved, painstaking, complicated, extensive, complex, careful → 24, 32, 34, 46, 48

elbow room: leeway, room for manoeuvre → 27, 29

embarrassment: awkwardness, discomfort, distress, confusion, agitation → 13

emphasising: underlining, underscoring, accentuating → 27-28, 154

endurance: staying power, perseverance, tenacity, fortitude, stamina → 37, 39, 101

enlightening: informative, revealing, helpful, instructive, useful → 146

ensuing: following, subsequent, resulting, succeeding, later → 8-9, 22, 25

entire: whole, complete, full, total → 21-22, 24

entrepreneurial: corporate, business, company. commercial → 35, 38

environment: situation, surroundings, setting, milieu, background, circumstances → 8, 144, 146-148

erroneously: incorrectly, wrongly, inaccurately, mistakenly, fallaciously → 149, 152

error: mistake, inaccuracy, miscalculation, flaw, fault, misconception → 5, 92, 156-157

esteemed: respected, admired, valued, honoured, revered, highly thought of → 58-59, 136, 153-154

evaluation: assessment, appraisal, estimation

everything from one source: all from the same supplier or originator → 101

exception to the rule: exemption from the usual proceedings, exceptional case → 64, 67

expectations: outlook, speculation, prospects, hopes, viewpoint → 32, 34

exploratory talk: fact-finding or investigative conversation → 58-60, 69

extended: stretched out, outstretched, spread out → 142-143

extension: call-through, direct dial, direct access → 54, 56

extension to the building: addition, add-on, supplement, or augmentation to the structure → 8, 10, 46-48

extensive: comprehensive, wide-ranging, thorough, large-scale, substantial, considerable → 8, 10

exterior: outward, outer, external → 55, 77, 109, 126-127, 140

extras: optional or special equipment → 115, 117

faded: dull, pale, discoloured, washed out → 52, 80-81

failure: defeat, fiasco, blunder, shortfall, flop, loss → 112, 114

fashion: way, manner, mode, method → 73-75, 116

fast pace: high rate of progress, tempo, or momentum → 11, 13, 91

fast-paced: hurried, hasty, fleet-footed, accelerated, brisk → 36, 38

fear: worry, concern, misgiving, unease, dread → 69-70

final: definitive, definite, absolute, irrevocable → 43, 45, 84, 125, 135

firm order of events: definite or fixed sequence on how to proceed → 23, 82, 98-100, 111

flexible work time: adaptable working hours, flexitime → 21, 24

forces: strengths, powers, strong points, assets, plus points → 40, 42

foreman: overseer, supervisor, chief → 48, 70

foremost: leading, principal, top, primary, most important, chief, prime → 53, 55

frame: condition, state, situation, circumstance → 60

free space: leeway, freedom, flexibility, room to manoeuvre → 17, 102, 104

frequently: often, many times, repeatedly, over and over, continually, constantly, habitually → 109-110

friction: hostility, tension, conflict, quarrelling, arguing, bickering → 41

from rural areas: from the countryside, from agricultural regions → 87, 89

fuel: stimulus, incentive, encouragement → 35, 38

furniture and fixtures: furnishings and fittings → 6-7

future: upcoming, forthcoming, expected, yet to come → 35-37, 43, 45, 47, 58, 74, 99, 102-103

gain: benefit, advantage, reward, profit → 7, 12, 14, 20, 32, 67, 70, 104, 110, 124, 140-141, 144, 153

gateway: bridge. link, connection, tie → 38

gaze: look, stare, gape → 17-19

gender: sex, masculinity or femininity → 80-81

generous: giving, open-handed → 54, 56

genuine: indisputable, true, actual, legitimate, real, valid, authentic → 10, 118, 120, 135

gossip: rumours, idle talk, hearsay, smear campaign → 12, 14

grace period: timeframe in which protection is granted, temporary immunity → 32, 34

gratuitously: needlessly, pointlessly, senselessly → 91-93

guild: line of work, profession, line of business → 52-53, 55

guilty party: blameworthy or culpable persons → 91, 93

hardly any: barely any, scarcely any, almost no → 91-92

harmful: unsafe, damaging, injurious, risky, dangerous, toxic, destructive → 49, 51, 88-90

has determined: has found out, learned, experienced, or discovered → 84, 95-96

has to be geared towards: has to be aimed or directed towards → 150, 152

hazardous: unsafe, perilous, harmful → 87, 89

head of engineering: person in charge or in command of manufacturing → 53, 55-56

health advisory service on environ-mentally compatible building materials: consultative facility on ecologically sound or non-polluting construction resources → 89

high-maintenance: demanding, challenging, taxing → 151

high-profile: impressive, imposing, daunting, commanding, arresting → 19-20

high risk of failure: strong chance for breakdown, stoppage, or non-function → 73, 75

host: organiser, one who furnishes facilities for a function or event → 87, 89

idiosyncrasy: peculiarity, individual trait, habit → 116

impartial: unbiased, neutral, balanced, fair-minded, open-minded, objective → 147, 149

imperative: very important, crucial, necessary, indispensable, vital, essential → 140-141, 144, 153-154

implementation: carrying out, realisation, enforcement, execution, fulfillment, pushing through, application → 70

implications: repercussions, effects, impact, outcome → 73, 75

in accordance with: in agreement, conformity, or compliance with → 119, 121

in advance: beforehand, prior, ahead of time, earlier → 74, 84, 100

in an instant: instantly, at once, in no time, directly, right away, promptly → 134-135

in depth: thoroughly, extensively, comprehensive, in detail → 99, 101

in favour of: for, in support of, on behalf of, pro, on the side of, giving backing to → 98, 100

in making something reach its peak: in causing something to arrive at or get to its highest point → 25

in particular: especially, particularly, specifically → 153

in regard to: on the subject of, as to, concerning, on the matter of → 22, 150

in the preliminary stage: in the introductory, beginning, or opening phase → 10, 13

in vain: futile, unsuccessful, unavailing → 79, 81, 95-96

incidentally: by the way, while we're on the subject, before I forget → 6-7

inciting: encouraging, stimulating, provoking, arousing, inflaming → 36, 38

indeed: in fact, rightly, actually, positively, for sure → 11, 72, 91, 97

independent of: regardless of, notwithstanding, irrespective of → 131-132

in-depth: thorough, detailed, comprehensive, extensive, profound → 52

indispensable: essential, necessary, high-priority, fundamental, key → 140-141

industrious: hardworking, productive, busy, conscientious, diligent, active → 52-53, 55

inexpertly: clumsily, ineptly, tactlessly → 11, 13

influential: powerful, important, high-ranking, leading → 58, 80, 97, 100, 135, 148

inhibition: reservation, qualms, hesitancy, doubt, restraint, hang-ups, shyness, self-consciousness → 110-113, 126-127

initial: first, early, preliminary → 7, 11, 19, 23, 26, 43, 45, 86, 91, 109, 150-151, 153

initial stage: start-up period, early stage, opening → 151, 153

initially: first of all, at first, in the first instance → 111

innocent victim: a person who pretends to have been wronged → 129-130

insignificant: unimportant, irrelevant, uninfluential, powerless → 112, 124, 137, 140-141

instance: case, example, case in point → 16

instant: immediate, on-the-spot, direct, prompt, instantaneous → 134-135

instead of: as an alternative to, as a substitute for, as a replacement for → 20, 27, 33, 53, 70, 76, 88, 109

interest: dividend, profit, return. percentage gain → 23, 54, 66, 90, 108-109, 122

interfering: bothersome, annoying, irritating, disruptive → 60-61

interpersonal relationships: human relations → 151, 153

interposed questions: placed-between, interjected, or inserted queries → 12, 14

introductory: initial, starting, preliminary, opening → 6-7, 13, 84, 86

involved: associated, participating → 24, 27, 34, 40, 42-44, 48, 58, 60, 68, 88, 100, 127, 133, 145

involvement: engagement, commitment → 76-78

is available: is to be had, is on hand, is obtainable, is existing → 94

is depreciated: is devalued, downgraded, reduced, diminished, or minimised → 11, 13

is flogged to death: is used way too much or too often → 9

is mistaken for: is confused with, mixed up with, or misinterpreted as → 109-110

is quoted: is cited, given, or named → 21, 24

is rewarded properly: is recompensed or compensated appropriately → 37-38

issue: question, subject, matter, topic → 40, 42, 52, 65-66, 87, 89, 100, 152, 155

it can be determined: it can be verified, ascertained, or established → 80, 82

joint: common, shared, combined, collective, cooperative, consolidated, concerted → 120-121

judgement: common sense, good sense, perception, wisdom, understanding → 59, 81, 133, 135

judging by your look: guessing, assessing, surmising, or guesstimating by your gaze → 16, 18

key: crucial, vital, critical, decisive, important, influential, significant → 7, 26, 44, 46-47, 49, 91-92, 110, 118-120, 133, 135, 141, 149-152

key account: profitable, lucrative, moneymaking, major, or important customer → 26, 47, 118-120, 149-152

knowledge for the sake of control: information withheld by superiors → 32, 34

lack of: absence of, need of, deficiency in, shortage of, insufficiency in, absence, deprivation → 32, 34, 102, 104

lapse: slip, error, mistake, blunder → 92

largely: for the most part, basically, to a large extent, to a great degree, mainly, mostly, essentially, by and large → 17, 83, 85

lavish: elaborate, involved, highly structured, complex, extravagant → 21, 24

lead: hint, suggestion, recommendation, information, pointer, tip, suggestion, pointer, clue → 46, 53-55, 60, 67, 78-80, 85, 150

lecture: talk, address, speech, discourse, lesson → 88-89

leeway: room to manoeuvre, room to operate, elbowroom, freedom, flexibility → 29, 110

leisure time: free time, spare time, time off → 153

less obvious: not so noticeable, apparent, or evident → 80, 82

line of business: area of trade, field of commerce → 55, 99, 101

link: connection, relation, tie, bond → 38, 44-46, 57-58, 81, 92, 124

lively: energetic, animated, enthusiastic, high-spirited, stimulating, exciting, active → 11, 14, 25

lone fighter: solary, companionless, unaccompanied, or single combatant → 48

long drawn-out: stretched out, dragged out, protracted, lengthy → 68-69

loss: leaving, departure, disappearance → 16, 18, 111, 113, 116, 136

low-maintenance: undemanding, easy to care for or get along with → 149, 152

low profit contribution: scarce contribution margin, product profitability, or profit margin → 118, 120-121

main: major, chief, principal, most important → 23, 33, 51, 58, 102, 148, 155

mainly: largely, chiefly, mostly, for the most part, primarily, chiefly, principally → 59, 70-71, 85, 144

major: bigger, greater, important, weighty, prime → 12, 16, 95-96, 108, 135, 152

marry in haste, repent at leisure: if you do something in a hurry, you may regret it for a long time → 150, 152

mastermind: prime mover, architect, engineer, author, originator → 38

matching: appropriate, compatible, fitting, applicable, proper, suitable, consistent, corresponding, complementing, equivalent, parallel, analogous, to go with, to complement, to harmonise with → 77-78, 102

matter: issue, question, problem, topic, subject, affair, situation, circumstance→ 8-9, 11, 26, 50, 52, 66, 89, 100, 102, 109, 111, 115-117, 122-123, 129, 131, 133, 154

matter-of-factly: factually, straightforwardly → 41-42

may be doomed: could be disaster-prone, ill-fated, or ruined → 8-9

measure: step, action, move → 59, 77, 79, 81, 90, 128-129, 137, 157

measures: actions, courses of action, proceedings, steps, means, activities, course of action, ways, methods, channels, instruments → 75, 77-78, 88, 111, 113, 119, 126, 155

mechanical engineering company: machine or engine-building firm → 46, 57, 59

mediator: go-between, intermediary, facilitator, middleman, liaison, third party → 57-59, 148

merely: just, only, simply, nothing more than, purely → 99, 101, 120, 122-123, 156-157

merging as: coming together, joining together, joining forces, or uniting as → 47-48

mindset: state of mind, frame of mind, way of thinking, attitude, mentality → 15, 17

minor: small, insignificant, negligible → 122-124, 137

minor detail: inconsequential, trivial, small, unimportant, or insignificant aspect → 122-124

miserly: tight-fisted, penny-pinching, stingy, closefisted, parsimonious, tight, ungenerous → 112, 114

mistake: blunder, inaccuracy, miscalculation, slip-up → 84, 91-93, 157

more probing: more detailed, in-depth, or penetrating → 50, 52

most promising: best, the most favourable, auspicious, or positive → 87, 89, 109-110

mountaineer: rock climber, hiker → 37, 39

much greater challenge: much more difficult task or venture → 43, 45

multifaceted: many-sided, versatile, manifold, all-round, varied, diverse → 47-48

mumbling: muttering, murmuring → 27-28

negotiation: bargaining, discussion → 26, 28, 126

nevertheless: all the same, just the same, in any event, nonetheless → 92, 116

new guy: newcomer, the beginner, the new arrival → 144-146

nit-picker: faultfinder, knocker, whiner → 129-130

nonchalantly: imperturbably, collected, indifferent, casual, insouciant, laid-back → 33, 35

not suffer from it: not be affected, afflicted, or troubled by it → 91-92

not to mention: not counting, not including, to say nothing of, in addition to → 77, 79

objection: counterargument, opposition → 23-24, 90, 128

objective: goal, intention, purpose → 23, 25, 37, 119, 149

obliged: required, obligated, called-for, compelled → 155

obstacle: hindrance, complication, problem, hurdle → 43, 45, 95

obvious: apparent, visible, noticeable, clear, evident, perceptible, palpable, discernible, recognisable → 22, 80, 82, 108, 150, 153

occasion: event, occurrence, circumstance → 95

occupation: activity, work, profession, job, field, trade → 86, 89

of all concerned: of everyone involved or implicated → 40, 42

of one's own accord: of one's own free will, voluntarily, freely, willingly → 100, 130

of that magnitude: of that scale, degree, or size → 99, 101

on behalf of: for, representing, as a representative of, in the interests of → 54, 56, 100

on difficult terrain: under demanding circumstances, under tough conditions → 86, 89

on what terms they are with someone: what their standing or relationship is with someone → 146

one is dealt a blow: one experiences a setback, disappointment, misfortune, or knock-back → 113

one-of-a-kind: singular, unrivalled, first tate, first class, supreme → 35, 38

opinion poll: survey, review, sample, market research → 152

opinion-forming: point of view-shaping or determining → 58-59

opportune: appropriate, favourable, apt, suitable, fitting → 55, 100

order of precedence: sequence or classification of priority → 23, 25

outdated: obsolete, out of date, antiquated, superseded, old-fashioned → 83-85

outside observer: uninvolved watcher, onlooker, eyewitness, or bystander → 52, 55

outside supplier: subcontractor, component supplier → 94, 96

outstanding: exceptional, terrific, excellent, great → 13

overall sales: general or total selling → 118-120

overheard: listened in on, eavesdropped on → 53, 55

owner: possessor, holder, keeper → 21, 67, 103, 135

ownership: possession, control, command → 133, 136

pain: hurting, suffering, unhappiness → 90

palm of one's hand: under part of the hand between the fingers and the wrist → 19

paper: treatise, study, report, analysis → 100

paragraph: section, subdivision, segment → 68-69

particular: specific, individual → 32, 67, 115, 134, 153

particularities: individual characteristics, features, or attributes → 64, 67

past: previous, preceding, last → 41, 124, 142, 144

path: way, road, avenue, route → 71

peak performance: top accomplishment or achievement → 39

perceived: sensed, felt → 17, 19, 93

perseverance: persistence, determination, resoluteness, insistence, tenacity → 39, 115-116

persuasive: compelling, convincing, gripping, effective → 68-69

pertaining to: affecting, concerning, regarding, relating to, applying to, having a relevance to, being relevant to → 32, 34, 60-61, 89, 156-157

physical discomfort: bodily ache, pain, soreness, tenderness, or irritation → 88, 90

pitfall: trap, stumbling block, hazard, peril, danger, difficulty → 13

pleasant: friendly, nice, enjoyable, pleasurable, pleasing → 8-9, 140-141

pleasantly: in a friendly way, politely, agreeably, in a charming way, amiably → 76, 78, 116-117

pollution: contamination, smog, effluence, adulteration → 87-89

possibly: perhaps, maybe, for all one knows → 15, 17, 19

praise: applause, acclaim, approval, acclamation, commendation → 12, 14

preconceived: predetermined, prearranged, predecided → 26, 28

predecessor: precursor, forerunner → 144-145

predetermined: fixed, set, prearranged, preagreed, predecided, preplanned, preset → 28, 142-143

predetermined duration: fixed, prearranged, or preset period → 142-143

prediction: forecast, calculation → 80-81

prejudice: bias, narrow-mindedness, discrimination, intolerance, unfairness, prejudgement, preconception, bias, predisposition → 34, 143

premise: idea, precondition, prerequisite → 12, 14

premises: grounds, building, location, property, place → 53, 55

prerequisite: circumstance, situation, condition, precondition, requisite, necessity, essential, qualification, requirement → 14, 83, 85, 87, 89, 98, 101-102, 104

presence: being there, company → 19-20, 77, 109, 122-123

present: current, existing, present-day, contemporary → 8, 22, 27, 33, 44, 56, 59-60, 66, 73-74, 83, 85, 97, 99-100, 103, 105, 108, 113, 117, 140, 148

pretext: excuse, alleged reason, pretence, cover → 108

previous: earlier, preceding, prior → 76

previously: before, until that time, earlier on, in the past, formerly, until then, once, at one time → 87, 123-124, 146

primarily: above all, mainly, for the most part, mostly, in the first place → 58-59, 153

principal: most important, chief, main, most influential, leading → 51, 60, 147-148

probability: likelihood, possibility, odds → 79-81

proceedings: measures, procedures, courses of action → 34

processing speed: operational pace → 54, 56

promising: encouraging, hopeful → 87, 89, 109-110

promptness: speediness, rapidity, swiftness, quickness → 117-118

prospective customer: potential, future, likely, or soon-to-be client → 96

prospects: potential, possibilities, promise, expectations → 59-61, 80, 104, 149, 152

prospects for: likelihood or possibility of, chances for → 149, 152

provided: as long as, if, given, with the provision that, on the condition that, on the assumption that → 74, 76, 78, 104, 123-124, 153-154

provided that: as long as, on the condition that, with the provision that → 153-154

provider: supplier, source, contributor, bringer, giver → 54, 76, 83, 103

psychological strain: mental stress, emotional suffering, nervous tension, anxiety, mental pressure → 73, 75, 82-83, 85

public figure: celebrity, celebrated public character, very important person → 59

purely: simply, just, solely, entirely, completely, totally, wholly → 123, 132, 134, 157

purpose: use, function, task → 25, 41

purposefully: with determination, with, resolve, resolutely, single-mindedly → 36, 38, 121

pushy: aggressive, forceful, insistent, hard-line, overambitious → 19-20

quarrel: dispute, disagreement, clash, squabble, feud → 39, 41

questionnaire: opinion poll, survey → 150, 152

quirk: foible, oddity, hang-up, eccentricity → 116

range: assortment, variety, array, choice → 12, 50, 133, 150

rapport: understanding, affinity, harmony → 117, 152

rare: unusual, uncommon, out of the ordinary, exceptional → 95-96

rarely: hardly ever, seldom, not often → 154-155

rather: more exactly, more accurately → 80, 82, 111

ready cash: money in the pocket → 53, 55

really self-evident things: things that go without saying, the most natural things → 117

reasoning: way of thinking, interpretation, analysis, reckoning → 16, 18

recent: current, new, fresh, topical → 59-60

recently: just, a short time ago, lately, not long ago → 53, 55, 123-124

recipe: formula, method, procedure → 32, 34

reckoning: estimate, calculation scheme, weighing up → 18

recognised: appreciated, honoured, applauded, endorsed → 19, 32, 133, 136

recognition: acknowledgement, appreciation, applause → 79

recurring: frequent, constant, repeated, habitual, regular, continual, returning → 39-41, 82

referral: reference, recommendation, good word, testimonial → 58, 103, 105, 154

refusal: negative response, rejection, non-acceptance, no, thumbs down, negation → 74, 96-99

regarded as: thought of, viewed, or looked upon as → 26, 28

regardless: anyway, in any case, nevertheless, nonetheless, despite everything, no matter what, at any rate, anyhow → 16, 114-116, 132

related: connected, associated, accompanying, linked, correlated → 38, 72-74, 101

related to: connected with, linked to, associated with, affiliated with → 101

relating to: applying to, having relevance to, concerning, pertaining to → 34, 60, 87, 89, 157

reliable: dependable, trustworthy, well-founded, credible, sound → 14, 143

remarkable: extraordinary, exceptional, outstanding, noteworthy, phenomenal → 11, 13

removed: eliminated, taken away, done away with, eradicated → 97, 100, 110

remuneration: compensation, salary, payment → 114

repair shop: workshop, auto body shop → 67

repeated: recurring, repetitive, frequent → 41, 80, 82

repeatedly: frequently, time after time, again and again → 39, 41, 68

replacement: successor, substitute, stand-in, fill-in, proxy → 47, 54, 56, 66, 123, 144-145

replacement purchases: substitute or alternative acquisitions → 47, 54, 56

research establishment: investigation, fact-finding, or exploration institute → 59

resentment: hard feelings, bitterness, irritation, animosity → 39, 41

respective: particular, specific, individual → 15, 88

responsibility: liability, accountability, answerability → 12, 83-84, 88, 92, 120-121

responsiveness: receptiveness, sensitivity, openness, reaction → 18

retention: preservation, maintenance, loyalty → 103

revaluated: upgraded, more important → 27, 29

revealing: informative, enlightening, useful, helpful, educational → 18, 144, 146

revelation: eye-opener, a realisation → 145

revenue: income, return, yield → 121

room for improvement: potential for development, possibilities for enhancement → 57, 59

sadly: unfortunately, unluckily, alas → 36, 38

sales approach: selling method strategy, tactic, or style → 75, 78

sales pitch: push, plug, or advertisement for a product or service → 142-143

sample: example, model, representative type → 16

scheduling of appointments: setting up or arrangement of a meeting → 42-43, 45

security need: requirement, demand, or wish for safekeeping → 102, 104

seemingly: apparently, on the face of it, ostensibly, outwardly → 8, 22, 53, 55, 112, 140-141

selection: assortment, range, variety, choice, mixture → 52

self-actualisation: self-realisation, self-fulfillment → 36, 38

semi: half, partially, partly → 149

sensitive: delicate, easily damaged, vulnerable → 96, 136-137

set of tools: instruments → 70-71

several: a number of, some, a few → 8, 50, 65, 68, 82, 104, 156

shared: joint, multiparty, combined, common, · collective, concerted → 48, 121

shipping agency: forwarding or hauling company → 67

sign of wear: symptom or evidence of deterioration → 55

similar: comparable, alike, much the same, related → 21, 36, 98, 101, 127, 133

sincere: genuine, true, honest, unfeigned, unaffected, wholehearted, heartfelt, serious, earnest → 108, 133-135

sincere: honest, straightforward, plain-dealing, not deceitful → 108, 133-135

single-mindedly: determinedly, persistently, resolutely, tenaciously, steadfastly → 38, 58, 60

site: plant, factory → 53, 55

skilfully: competently, expertly, cleverly, capably, efficiently → 10, 13, 128, 130

skill: competence, capability, ability → 33, 35

skilled: able, good, accomplished, competent, capable, experienced, proficient, trained, expert, practised → 16-19, 57-58

slight: small, minor, little → 18, 124

smoothly: without a hitch, well, efficiently, slickly, effortlessly, easily → 42-43, 45, 130, 132

solicited: asked for, requested, applied for, or sought → 47-48

sophisticated: complicated, complex → 68-69

sound: solid, well-founded, well-grounded, concrete, valid → 22, 68, 89, 94, 96, 126, 128

source: resource, well, supply, fund → 36, 54, 56, 64, 67, 145, 151

spare part: replacement element, substitute component → 66

spare parts wholesaler: extra or replacement component trader → 122-123

spare time: leisure time, time off, free time → 151, 153

stable: solid, strong, long-lasting, secure, steady, firm → 121-123

stall: delaying tactics, a pretext, → 108

standing: status, position, reputation, rank → 54, 119, 121, 146, 157

state-of-the-art: high-tech, up to date, modern, advanced → 83, 85

staying power: endurance, stamina, fortitude, patience → 39, 99, 101

steady: regular, usual, customary, habitual → 17, 123, 142-143

stopgap: temporary solution or substitute, makeshift, fill-in, last resort → 9, 11, 13

straight: non-stop, without interruption or break → 144-145

stroke of luck: fortunate or opportune coincidence → 53, 55

structurally completed home: bare brickwork house, building shell → 105

stuff that dreams are made of: things that visions, or imaginings consist of → 36, 38

subsequent: consecutive, successive, following, succeeding, later → 9, 25

substantial: sizable, generous, significant, real, weighty, major → 55

substantiated: backed up, validated → 74, 79, 81

subtle distinction: fine, fine-drawn, slight, minute, or tenuous difference → 16-18

sufficient: adequate, enough, plenty, satisfactory, good enough → 14, 54, 56, 144, 146

suitable: appropriate, fitting, pertinent → 6, 8, 58, 84, 86, 88, 111, 132, 157

superior objectives: higher goals, ambitions, intentions, targets, or ideas → 69-70

supposed to: meant, intended, expected to → 74-75

supposedly: allegedly, reputedly, theoretically → 33, 35

surfacing: emerging, appearing, materialising, developing → 91-92

surroundings: environment, setting, milieu, situation, environs, background, setting → 8-10, 144, 146, 148

survey: opinion poll, review, analysis → 152

tailor-made: custom-made, specially made, made to order, made to measure → 57, 59

tailored to: customised for, designed for, adapted to, modified for, adjusted to → 84, 86

tangible: touchable, palpable, tactile, visible → 86, 89

tardily: unpunctually, belatedly, slowly → 91-92

task: assignment, challenge, job, duty, chore → 33, 35, 39-41, 45, 56, 155

tension: worry, nervousness, apprehension, agitation → 22-23, 25, 41, 82, 85

terms: conditions, stipulations, specifications, provisions → 36, 39, 145-146, 156

territory: area, section, route → 49, 61

that need to be taken into account: that must be taken into consideration or kept in mind → 60

there is no clear-cut dividing line: the boundaries are undefined, vague, or non-specific → 9-10

this entails: this involves, requires, calls for, or necessitates → 102, 109-110

thorough: in-depth, exhaustive, systematic, comprehensive, intensive → 50-52, 111, 127

thoughtless: unthinking, unmindful, unwise, heedless, careless → 125, 127

to a bare minimum: to the smallest, least, or lowest degree → 16, 18

to abide by: to follow, to keep to → 42, 127

to accelerate: to step up, to speed up, to quicken, to expedite → 42

to accentuate: to emphasise, to highlight, to underline, to stress → 45, 136

to accompany: to go along with, to go together with, to escort, to come with, to go with → 48, 67, 116

to accomplish: to achieve, to get done, to realise, to bring about, to succeed in, to pull off → 20, 110, 121

to achieve: to accomplish, to pull off, to arrive at, to attain, to procure, to reach, to realise, to gain, to earn, to get → 20, 45, 104, 110, 121

to acknowledge: to recognise, to admit, to accept, to show appreciation for, to attach importance to → 7, 41

to act: to proceed, to operate, to work → 9, 41, 59, 95, 123

to act as: to serve as, to fulfill the function of, to do the work of a → 9, 59

to adapt: to change, to alter, to modify → 100, 116

to adapt to: to become accustomed to, to get a feel for, to get used to → 116

to address: to reach, to contact, to get in touch with, to get a message to → 16

to adhere to: to stick to, to abide by, to comply with, to follow, to cling to, to hold on to, to observe, to hold fast to, to be faithful to, to follow, to hold to, to fulfill, to stay with, to remain with, to not swerve from → 32, 34, 42, 127

to adjust: to adapt, to fine-tune, to align, to arrange, to orientate, to correct, to change, to alter, to modify, to amend → 39

to admit: to confess, to acknowledge, to reveal, to disclose, to divulge → 40-41

to advise: to give advice to, to counsel, to give an opinion to → 20, 46

to affect: to influence, to change, to alter → 39

to affirm: to confirm, to endorse, to support, to uphold → 135

to aid: to help, to support, to serve → 14

to aim: to aspire, to intend, to want → 70

to alert someone to something: to notify, inform, or warn someone about something → 145

to align something with something: to adjust or modify something to something → 38-39

to allege: to claim, to assert, to charge → 93, 130

to allot: to apportion, to allocate, to designate, to give, to appropriate → 25

to always move on the surface: to never go deep, to not be full of meaning → 10

to amplify: to strengthen, to augment → 38, 55

to appeal to someone: to go down well with someone, to attract someone → 118

to appear: to seem, to give the impression of being → 18, 86, 134

to appear aloof: to seem remote, distant, unapproachable, or detached → 18

to appear credible: to seem believable, trustworthy, convincing, or sincere → 134

to apply especially to: to be particularly relevant, pertinent, or significant to → 20, 110

to apply: to use, to exercise, to employ, to administer, to utilise, to put to use → 20-21, 28, 34, 60, 110

to appreciate: to value, to hold in high regard or esteem, to respect, to think highly of → 123, 127

to approach: to come up to, to talk to, to speak to, to deal with, to tackle, to handle, to set about, to make advances to, to make a proposal to, to proposition, to solicit, to handle, to speak to, to talk to, to get in touch with, to make contact with, to get in touch with → 76, 104

to arrive at: to come to, to reach, to attain, to make → 25, 45, 104, 110, 156-157

to assemble: to bring together, to put together, to round up, to collect → 48

to assert something: to maintain, support, or defend something → 35

to assess: to define, to determine, to establish, to consider, to evaluate, to judge, to appraise, to weigh up, to rate → 16, 18, 95, 113-114, 152

to assign: to allocate, to dole out, to distribute, to dispense, to apportion, to allot → 25, 93

to assume: to take for granted, to presume, to suppose, to presuppose, to believe, to imagine, to take up, to take on, to adopt, to come to have → 69, 83, 85

to assure: to promise to, to declare to, to affirm to, to give one's word to → 38

to attach great importance to something: to think or consider something to be essential → 104

to attain: to reach, to achieve, to accomplish, to obtain, to arrive at, to earn, to gain → 20, 45, 85, 104, 110, 157

to attend to: to take care of, to deal with, to give one's attention to, to see to, to focus on, to handle, to look after → 105, 120-121, 148

to attend: to be present at, to go to, to visit, to turn up at → 105, 120-121, 148

to attest: to authenticate, to prove, to confirm, to certify, to ratify, to validate → 127, 135

to attract attention: to create awareness, to draw interest or regard → 89-90

to avoid: to keep away from, to steer, to steer clear of, to shun → 49, 51, 91, 99, 101, 142

to awaken: to insire, to arouse, to prompt, to ignite → 25, 38

to bad-mouth someone: to put someone down, to backbite or trash someone → 93

to bad-mouth something: to speak critically or harshly of something → 130

to back something: to stand by, side with, support, or endorse something → 46

to be a giveaway: to be revealing, disclosing, divulging, or betraying → 18

to be a match for someone: to be an equal, an equivalent, or a peer for someone → 126

to be able to access: to be able to get into, gain access to, or fall back on → 141

to be affected by something: to be hit or afflicted by something → 7

to be an integral part: to be a basic, fundamental, or essential element → 104-105

to be annoyed: to be angry, frustrated, displeased, bothered, or exasperated → 96

to be applied: to be used, employed, utilised, or operated, put into practise, or brought into play → 24

to be assigned specifically: to be appointed, allocated, designated, or named purposefully → 121

to be assigned to someone: to be allocated, allotted, apportioned, or commissioned to someone → 51

to be at a loss: to be at one's wit's end, to be baffled, perplexed, puzzled, or bewildered → 18, 113

to be attended to: to be taken care of, dealt with, or given one's attention to → 78, 132

to be avoided at all costs: to be abstained from totally or completely → 7

to be aware of something: to be conscious of, informed of, or familiar with something → 100

to be aware of the fact: to be conscious of or sensitive to the reality → 96

to be banished: to be eliminated, dismissed, or removed → 110

to be banned from: to be expelled, barred, or excluded from → 21

to be called to account for something: to be requested to give reasons or show grounds for something → 86

to be common practise: to be everyday, routine, or standard procedure → 48

to be comparable to: to be like, equivalent to, or similar to → 127

to be compiled: to be assembled, put together, or brought together → 121

to be completely flabbergasted: to be totally stunned or shocked, to be left speechless → 41

to be completely rounded: to flow naturally and without interruption → 27-28

to be comprised of: to include, to consist of, to encompass → 68

to be confused with: to be mixed up with, to be mistaken for → 21

to be constantly worried: to be always anxious, nervous, or concerned → 127

to be convinced of something: to be positive, sure, or confident about something → 86

to be covered against something: to be insured against, provided for, or protected against something → 104

to be crucial: to be critical, essential, important, key, decisive, high-priority, or necessary → 141, 145

to be custom-tailored to: to be designed for, adapted to, or custom-made for → 66

to be cut down: to be limited, constrained, reduced, or restricted → 43, 45

to be divided into: to be split, separated, partitioned, or broken up into → 148

to be easily cajoled: to be talked into something with no trouble → 95-96

to be engaged in: to be involved in, busy with, or engrossed with → 145

to be entitled to something: to be given the right or be qualified to have something → 113

to be equipped with: to be fitted out, provided, furnished, or supplied with → 74

to be especially on guard: to be extra alert, vigilant, or watchful → 129-130

to be exhausted soon: to be used up, finished, or depleted before long → 127

to be extremely sensitive: to have keen senses, to be very receptive → 137

to be fine and dandy: to be all right, satisfactory, OK, or good → 132

to be fixated on someone: to be preoccupied or engrossed with someone → 123

to be forced on someone: to be pushed on someone, to be thrust down someone's throat → 110

to be fully justified by: to be completely acceptable or reasonable because of → 28

to be furnished with: to be outfitted or fitted out with → 114

to be geared towards: to be aimed at, to work toward → 150, 152

to be highly esteemed: to be greatly respected, regarded, or valued → 154

to be imperative: to be very important, vital, crucial, or necessary → 154

to be in a hurry: to be rushed, to have little or no time → 95

to be in for a surprise: to experience a bolt from the blue or a revelation → 145

to be in line with: to be in accord, in step, in conformity, or in rapport with → 149, 152

to be in vain: to be unsuccessful, ineffective, useless, futile, or unproductive → 79, 81

to be incorporated: to be included or integrated → 81-82

to be indispensable: to be crucial, vital, essential, very important, or key → 141

to be key: to be important, crucial, vital, or critical → 46

to be lacking: to not have, to be short of, to be deficient in → 126

to be much more favourable: to be much better, to be much more beneficial → 130

to be naturally imbedded in something: to be an normal part or element of something → 28

to be not more inclined to do something: to be not more prone, of a mind, apt, or disposed to do something → 82

to be nurtured: to be attended to, cultivated, cared for, or looked after → 131-132

to be on the lookout for: to be in search for or pursuit of → 56

to be outsourced: to be subcontracted, contracted out, or delegated → 45

to be part of something: to be associated with or involved in something → 127

to be perceived as trustworthy: to be professed, alleged, recognised, or understood as honest → 19

to be pleased to help one along: to be happy, delighted, or glad to assist one → 148

to be pressed for time: to be short of, have barely enough, or too little time → 95

to be proud of something: to be pleased with, happy about, appreciative of, or satisfied with something → 105

to be put to the test: to be tested, assessed, evaluated, or scrutinised → 126

to be resolved: to be sorted out, settled, or worked out → 150

to be responsive to something: to be open or quick to respond to something → 21

to be suitable: to be appropriate, fitting, apt, or right → 86

to be suited alike: to be appropriate, right, or qualified in the same way → 59

to be suited for something: to be appropriate, right, apt, or fitting for something → 132

to be tailored to: to be modified, customised, adapted, or adjusted to → 86

to be taken into account: to be considered, to be taken into consideration → 60, 81

to be taken under someone's wing: to be protected, looked after, or watched over by someone → 127

to be the most promising: to be the most favourable, to show the greatest potential → 89

to be thrilled: to be delighted, especially pleased, or very enthusiastic → 138

to be too focused on someone: to be too attached to or emotionally involved with someone → 68

to be tremendously accommodating: to be exceptionally obliging or cooperative → 138

to be truly convinced of something: to be really positive, confident, certain, or sure about something → 134

to be very much in tune with something: to be in accord, harmony, or concurrence with something → 67

to be worthwhile: to be sensible, advisable, worth the effort, or useful → 100

to bear cost-effectiveness in mind: to think economically, to remember to save expenses → 79, 81

to beat about the bush: to play for time, to use delaying tactics, to drag one's feet → 91-92

to become aware of: to know, to be informed of or in the know about something, to consciously register, to realise, to open one's eyes to → 48, 114

to become embarrassing: to become uncomfortable, discomforting, or awkward → 155

to become obvious: to become clear, apparent, recognisable, evident, or noticeable → 153

to blame: to point the finger at, to accuse, to assign fault to, to condemn → 93

to bond: to connect, to get on, to hit it off, to get along → 124

to boost: to increase, to expand, to raise, to add to, to improve, to amplify → 55, 104, 141

to bother: to concern, to perturb, to worry, to disconcert, to distress, to disturb, to trouble, to upset, to distress, to trouble → 42, 137

to brief: to inform, to prepare, to instruct, to fill in, to update, to advise → 46

to bring in line: to accommodate, to harmonise → 42

to bring something into play: to bring something up, to start talking about something → 114

to broach: to bring up, to introduce, to raise, to mention, to open → 101, 154-155

to build up tension: to create stress, nervousness, or apprehensiveness → 25

to call it a day: to finish or knock off work → 42

to call on: to appeal to, to ask, to request, to urge → 78

to calm someone down: to pacify, soothe, or appease someone → 130

to capture: to win over, to secure, to gain, to catch, to grab hold of → 153

to carry out: to fulfill, to complete, to execute, to finish → 74

to catch: to encounter, to come across, to come upon → 132, 153

to cause one a lot of grievance: to bring one a great deal of distress or anguish → 130

to cause one considerable anguish: to trigger a great deal of suffering or distress in one → 113

to check out: to look into, to take a look at, to examine, to research → 105

to choose: to decide on, to opt for, to go for, to select, to pick out, to settle on, to designate → 8, 89-90, 151, 157

to claim: to maintain, to argue, to assert, to declare, to profess, to allege → 93, 130

to clearly come into play: to unmistakeably stand out, show up, or catch the eye → 100

to cling to: to stick to, to hold to, to abide by, to adhere to → 34

to coax someone out of one's shell: to draw someone out, to induce someone to talk, to put someone at ease → 18

to coerce: to force, to pressure, to bully → 20

to come about: to happen, to occur, to crop up, to take place → 101, 127

to come across as: to be perceived or understood as → 93

to come out of one's shell: to loosen up, to relax, to become responsive → 14

to commence: to begin, to start, to get going → 10, 14

to commit: to promise, to vow, to give one's word, to pledge → 42, 152

to commit oneself to: to bind, promise, dedicate, or obligate oneself to → 152

to complain: to protest, to find fault, to object, to carp, to make a fuss → 104

to complement: to go well with, to be the perfect addition to → 78

to compose: to create, to write, to compile, to make up, to think up, to formulate → 71, 100, 154-155

to comprise: to include, to consist of, to contain, to be composed of, to make up, to form, to constitute, to compose → 71, 104

to conceal: to hide, to keep the lid on, to screen, to cover up → 92-93

to concern: to affect, to relate to, to involve, to be about, to have to do with, to pertain to → 42, 137

to conduct: to do, to carry out, to perform, to handle → 74

to confer: to have a consultation, to exchange views, to parley, to deliberate → 34-35

to confer obligingly: to discuss engagingly or bindingly → 34-35

to congratulate someone: to compliment or offer good wishes to someone → 143

to consider: to bear in mind, to take into account, to remember, to think about, to contemplate, to weigh up, to give thought to, to ponder → 25, 83, 101, 132, 134, 143

to consist of: to be made up of, to be formed of, to comprise, to contain, to include, to involve, to entail, to be composed of → 56, 68, 104

to constitute: to amount to, to represent, to signify, to be regarded as, to be equivalent to, to comprise, to create, to cause to be, to add up to → 71, 85-86

to contain: to hold, to include, to comprise, to involve, to incorporate → 104, 146

to contain oneself: to hold oneself back, to restrain oneself, to keep oneself in check, to control oneself → 146

to contemplate: to consider, to plan, to think about, to intend, to give thought to → 25, 132, 134

to contribute one's share: to do one's bit, to play one's part → 141

to contribute to: to be a factor in, to be conducive to, to lead to, to be instrumental in, to collaborate on, to work on, to play a role, to be a factor, to play a part → 9, 59, 78

to convey: to communicate, to express, to put across, to make known, to impart, to get across, to suggest → 28, 49, 51, 110, 113

to convince: to persuade, to prevail upon, to sway, to coerce, to win over, to influence, to bring around → 21, 24, 67, 78, 98, 100-101

to convince one to do otherwise: to persuade or influence one to reconsider → 100-101

to count: to matter, to be of consequence, to be of account, to make a difference → 78, 123

to count on: to trust in, to believe in → 78

to count more than: to matter more, be more important or significant than → 123

to cover: to include, to deal with, to contain, to comprise, to involve → 91, 93

to cover up: to conceal, to hide, to keep secret, to hush up, to keep dark → 91, 93

to crop up: to happen, to occur, to come to pass, to arise → 101

to dawdle: to waste or kill time, to idle, to linger, to dilly-dally → 55

to dawn on one: to occur to one, to register with one, to enter or cross one's mind → 114

to deal with something: to cope with, take care of, handle, or manage something → 101

to decline: to drop, to decrease, to fall, to lessen, to decrease, to diminish, to wane → 113

to decline without further explanation: to say no without giving a reason → 113

to deepen: to intensify, to reinforce, to emphasize, to stress, to underline → 121

to delve into: to explore, to enquire into, to examine, to research → 67

to demand: to require, to call for, to necessitate, to involve, to need, to want, to cry out for → 9, 120

to depend on: to hinge on, to be contingent upon, subject to, based upon, or influenced by → 25, 34

to depend on someone: to rely on, count on, or bank on someone → 34

to depend upon: to be contingent upon, subject to, determined by, based on, or influenced by → 120

to derive: to get, to gain, to obtain → 141

to derive from: to get, gain, receive, or draw from → 141

to deserve: to be worthy of, to be entitled to, to have the right to, to qualify for → 120, 135

to deserve equal treatment: to be worthy of one and the same handling → 120

to desire: to want, to need, to fancy, to be bent on, to wish for, to long for, to set one's heart on → 25, 75

to destroy: to damage, to harm, to impair → 13

to detect: to discern, to make out, to spot, to distinguish, to identify, to catch, to become aware of, to notice, to recognise, to perceive, to sense → 19, 48, 55, 114, 156-157

to determine: to ascertain, to establish, to verify, to clarify, to define, to fix, to constitute, to decide, to find out about, to learn about, to find out, to identify, to find out, to discover, to learn, to reveal, to uncover, to settle on, to fix, to decide, to agree on → 18, 39, 41, 44, 50, 58, 65, 67, 72, 90, 102, 112, 114, 121

to differentiate: to distinguish, to make a distinction, to contrast → 121

to diminish: to take the edge off, to detract from, to belittle → 25, 93

to discern: to distinguish, to recognise, to perceive, to detect, to observe → 17, 19, 157

to disclose: to reveal, to make known, to divulge, to impart → 41, 135

to discover: to come across, to find, to detect, to encounter, to locate → 55

to dismantle something: to demolish or destroy something → 28

to display: to exhibit, to demonstrate → 19-20, 28, 77, 113

to disprove: to invalidate, to contradict, to negate, to refute, to challenge → 18, 128

to distract: to divert, to turn away, to avert, to sidetrack → 33, 35

to divert from something: to turn away or move away from something → 35

to do one's share: to do one's bit, to play one's part, to pitch in, to cooperate, to lend a hand → 46

to do the preliminary work: to do the groundwork or first round → 155

to drag out: to protract, to prolong, to draw out, to delay, to stretch out, to extend → 113

to draw a conclusion: to deduce, infer, conclude, derive, or gather something → 112, 114

to draw the conclusion: to take the necessary steps → 148

to draw up: to compose, to formulate, to write out, to put down on paper, to work out, to create, to think up, to devise → 100, 121

to drift into triteness: to become banal, commonplace, hackneyed, trivial, or prosaic → 74

to drop some appropriate cues: to intersperse some key words → 7

to ease: to relieve, to reduce, to lessen, to simplify, to facilitate, to expedite, to clear the way for, to help → 14, 121

to elapse: to pass, to go by, to slip by → 20-21, 101

to elongate: to make longer, to draw out, to extend, to stretch out → 92

to embellish: to embroider, to decorate, to adorn, to enhance, to enrich → 25

to emerge: to appear, to become visible, to surface, to materialise, to come out, to transpire, to occur → 86

to emphasise: to accentuate, to call attention to, to highlight, to give prominence to, to stress, to underline, to underscore, to underline → 45, 56, 69, 82, 116, 136, 155

to employ: to work with, to use, to make use of, utilise → 21, 101, 135

to encounter: to be faced with, to be confronted with, to come across or upon → 21, 55, 74, 132

to encourage: to persuade, to convince, to influence → 18, 34, 38, 67, 74

to endeavour on: to try one's hand at, to do one's best at, to make an effort at → 144, 146

to endure: to weather, to withstand, to stick out, to get through → 86

to enhance: to improve, to increase, to add to, to augment, to boost → 25

to enjoy doing something: to take pleasure in, get pleasure from, or like doing something → 148

to enjoy their effect to the fullest: to savour or relish their results thoroughly → 25

to enrol: to register, to sign up, to put one's name down → 76, 78

to ensue: to develop, to follow, to occur, to happen, to turn up, to transpire, to come to pass → 116

to ensure: to make sure, to make certain, to guarantee, to warrant → 38, 136

to entail: to involve, to require, to call for, to necessitate → 56, 104, 120

to enter: to mark down, to record, to register, to put down, to note → 44, 51, 114, 140-141

to envisage something: to imagine, foresee, visualise, picture, see, or anticipate something → 153

to envision: to envisage, to picture, to imagine, to picture, to see in one's mind's eye, to foresee, to visualise → 75, 96, 104, 134-135

to envision in one's mind: to visualise, picture, or foresee in one's thinking → 135

to exceed: to go beyond, to surpass, to beat, to top, to outdo → 86

to exchange: to swap, to trade, to barter → 140-141

to exclude: to leave out, to keep out, to bar, to shut out → 8-9

to experience: to go through, to encounter, to become familiar with → 21, 86, 145

to explore: to investigate, to examine, to look into, to inquire into → 67, 74, 96

to express: to demonstrate, to communicate, to exhibit, to indicate, to state, to say, to voice → 28, 96, 110, 113

to extend: to expand, to lengthen, to increase in length, to continue → 92, 113

to exude: to emanate, to display, to radiate, to ooze, to emit, to give off → 28, 113

to face someone: to deal with. handle, come to terms with, or meet someone → 39

to facilitate: to help, to assist, to aid, to advance, to ease, to smooth the path of, to make possible, to make easier, to make smoother → 11, 14, 71

to fall through: to come to nothing, to fail to happen, to not come off, to fall flat, to go awry, to fizzle out → 116

to feature: to include, to have, to present, to introduce, to highlight, to promote, to emphasise → 29, 56

to feel angry toward: to feel annoyed, irritated or infuriated toward → 41

to feel bound: to feel compelled, obliged, or obligated → 155

to feel flattered: to feel complimented, pleased, grateful, fawned-upon, or thrilled → 14

to feel very strongly about something: to get quite emotional, passionate, or fanatical over something → 9

to figure out: to understand, to comprehend, to make out, to see, to reason → 16, 58-60

to find it inappropriate: to think of it as improper, tasteless, unseemly, unfitting, or tactless → 113

to fizzle out: to peter out, to fade away, to come to an end, to disappear, to fold, to flop, to fall through → 116, 132

to force down: to apply pressure to reduce, lower, or cut → 26, 28

to force something down: to cut, lower, or reduce something → 114

to foresee: to anticipate, to predict → 75, 96

to fret about something: to worry about, make a fuss over, or feel peeved about something → 116

to function without a hitch: to go off or run smoothly, easily, trouble-free or effortlessly → 42, 132

to gain: to achieve, to arrive at, to pick up, to build up, to secure, to attain, to reach, to get, to win, to obtain, to capture, to pick up, to procure, to acquire → 7, 14, 20, 32, 104, 140-141, 153

to gather: to collect, to garner, to gain, to get together, to accumulate, to compile, to bring together, to round up, to put together → 7, 48, 143

to get accustomed to: to get used to, to become familiar with, to get adapted to → 144, 146

to get into: to start with, to get going with, to commence with, to instigate, to bring about → 10, 116, 141

to get one's way: to prevail, to come out on top, to get others to agree → 117

to get over something: to think no more of or come around from something → 101

to get something off the ground: to get something going or under way → 38

to get the subject across: to make one understand or become familiar with the topic → 88, 90

to give in to: to succumb to, to give way to, to go along with → 14

to give one that edge: to provide one with the advantage or upper hand → 117-118

to give oneself away: to reveal, divulge, or make known oneself → 114

to give proof: to produce evidence, verification, or confirmation → 78

to go haywire: to go wrong, to go out of control, to become disorganised → 96

to go off without a hitch: to go smoothly, to go without difficulties → 130

to go to great trouble over something: to go to great pains over or make a big effort in doing something → 82

to guide someone through something: to direct, steer, or lead someone through something → 85

to haggle the price down: to bargain or negotiate for lowering the cost by → 104-105

to happen to be away on holiday: to turn out to be on vacation → 68

to happen to be fortunate: to turn out to be lucky or successful → 145

to have a hotline to Heaven: to be intuitive, psychic, telepathic, or second sighted → 55

to have an edge on someone: to have an advantage or the lead on someone → 67

to have an impact on something: to influence or affect something, to have a bearing on something → 24

to have been a long time coming: to have been in the offing for an extended period → 137

to have fully adjusted to something: to have entirely gotten used or attuned to something → 143

to have gotten into the habit of doing something: to have started a routine or practice of doing something → 113

to have harmful effects on something: to have damaging results or consequences for something → 51

to have in common with someone: to do or experience similarly as someone → 124

to have something reconfirmed: to have something once again verified, substantiated, or validated → 74

to have succeeded: to have been successful or victorious → 25

to have to acquaint oneself intensely with: to have to familiarise oneself thoroughly with → 52

to have to be quoted: to have to be mentioned, cited, or given → 28

to have to broach the subject again: to have to bring up the issue another time → 155

to have trust in someone: to have faith, confidence, or belief in someone → 123

to highlight: to mark, to tag → 45, 56, 69, 82, 136

to impair: to damage, to harm, to spoil, to diminish → 24-25

to implement: to put into effect, to realise, to carry out, to execute, to put into practice, to apply, to employ → 60, 65

to imply: to signify, to mean, to indicate → 29

to impress: to make an impact on, to amaze, to astonish, to stir, to influence → 116, 146

to impress upon someone: to emphasise to, instil in, or bring home to someone → 116

to increase: to add to, to boost, to augment, to enhance, to heighten → 23, 45, 55, 73-74, 77, 119

to indicate: to be a sign, to signify, to show, to reveal, to imply → 29

to induce one: to provoke, prompt, inspire, or motivate one → 99

to interlink: to interconnect, to cross-link → 75

to internalise something: to assimilate something, to take something in → 67

to introduce one to: to present one to, to familiarise or acquaint one with → 148

to invoke: to bring into play, to quote, to cite, to use, to bring up, to state → 35

to join in: to participate in, to take part in, to contribute to, to partake in → 8-9

to judge: to assess, to evaluate, to perceive, to recognise, to comprehend, to estimate, to guess, to surmise, to guesstimate → 18, 93, 95, 114, 126, 152

to jump to: to immediately address, concentrate on, or take up → 74-75

to keep one's composure: to keep a stiff upper lip, one's poise, or one's self-possession → 116-117

to keep someone on tenterhooks intentionally: to keep someone hanging on purpose → 41

to keep something alive: to keep something thriving, active, or blooming → 132

to keep something available: to keep something on hand, obtainable, or ready → 79

to keep track of something: to keep up with, to follow, to monitor → 56

to keep up: to maintain, to sustain, to preserve, to uphold, to retain → 56

to land off the mark: to be off base or wide of the mark → 13

to lastingly secure: to continually ensure, assure, guarantee, or underwrite → 71

to leave: to give up or quit one's job at → 9, 65-66, 142-144

to let one day pass by: to allow 24 hours to elapse or go by → 101

to limit oneself to: to restrict or confine oneself to → 141

to liven up: to put some life into, to put some spark into, to add some zest to, to give a boost to → 69

to long for something: to yearn for, crave, desire, or wish for something → 85

to look into: to explore, to investigate, to research, to make inquires about → 74, 105

to mainly affect: to mostly have an effect on, influence, or have an impact on → 70-71

to maintain: to cultivate, to foster, to support, to encourage, to promote, to keep, to retain, to uphold, to sustain, to keep up, to preserve, to keep in existence → 34-35, 46, 93

to make a cut: to bring to an end, halt, stop, or discontinue (the small talk) → 10

to make another attempt: to try again, to make a new effort → 101

to make flimsy excuses: to make feeble, weak, poor, or thin pretences → 96

to make good sense: to be a good idea, practical, or useful → 101

to make it a habit: to make it a rule, routine, or pattern → 141

to make something accessible to someone: to make something understandable or comprehensible to someone → 89

to make the difference: to decide the issue, to clinch matters → 66

to mark: to indicate, to point to, to show → 51

to master the art of something: to become proficient, skilled, or adept in something → 18

to match: to fill into, to go with, to belong to → 101

to matter: to be of importance, to count, to be significant → 123

to measure: to determine the length, width, and height of → 59, 90

to meet: to fulfill, to satisfy, to fill → 14, 53, 55, 74

to memorise the fine print: to remember or learn by heart the small lettering → 129-130

to mention: to talk about, to bring up, to call attention to, to point out, to state, to refer to → 9, 15, 77, 79, 108

to monitor: to keep an eye on, to keep track of, to check, to oversee → 56, 138

to move forward with someone: to make headway, make progress, or gain ground with someone → 67

to neglect: to fail to look after, to be lax about, to pay little or no attention to → 131-132

to not arise: to not come up, occur, happen, develop, or come to pass → 137

to not be able to complain about: to not be able to grumble, grouse, moan, or lament about → 104

to not be trustworthy: to not be reliable, dependable, or honourable → 14

to not beat about the bush: to get down to business immediately → 96

to not leave it at: to not end it or stop at → 56

to not materialise: to not come into being, happen, occur, or come about → 90, 100

to not proceed according to plan: to not continue in line with the strategy → 24

to not regard: to not look upon, consider, see, deem, or think of → 123

to not slip into: to not change to, to not go downhill to, to not deteriorate into → 7

to not waver: to not falter, to not hesitate, to not become unsteady → 101

to nourish: to encourage, to further, to advance, to promote → 38

to nudge someone onto something: to gently push or urge someone onto something → 105

to nurture: to cultivate, to develop, to support, to boost, to advance → 140-141

to obtain: to get, to attain, to acquire, to pick up, to get hold of → 14, 20, 58, 83, 85, 110, 141

to occur: to happen, to come about, to come to pass
→ 86, 101, 114, 127

to offer benefit: to provide advantage, to give
assistance, to furnish gain → 110

to offer compensation: to make amends, to put
forward reparation or recompense → 92-93

to outshine: to outdo, to surpass, to put in the shade,
to tower above → 23, 25

to overrate: to overestimate, to think too much of,
to place too much emphasis on, to attach too much
importance to → 19

to oversee: to supervise, to run, to watch over,
to manage, to direct → 138

to own: to be the owner of, to have possession of,
to possess, to have → 23, 134-135

to paint a clear picture of something: to delineate,
define, describe, outline, or portray something → 135

to paint a vivid picture of something: to make
something crystal-clear → 75

to pass on: to convey, to forward, to impart, to
communicate, to transmit, to send, to dispatch → 59

to pay: to be worth one's while or worth it → 17, 19,
42, 55, 76, 79, 81, 94, 96, 132

to pay dearly for something: to be punished for
or atone for something → 96

to pay off: to meet with success, to get results, to be
effective or profitable → 55

**to pay the same degree of attention to each
prospect:** to concentrate one's efforts equally on each
potential client → 79, 81

to perceive: to recognise, to distinguish, to make out,
to identify, to detect, to sense, to feel, to understand
→ 19, 67, 85, 95, 114, 137

to persuade someone to do something: to convince,
sway, or induce someone to do something → 78

to peruse: to read thoroughly or carefully, to examine,
to scrutinise, to check → 152-153

to pick up the thread: to develop a thought further,
to spin a thought out, to expand on an idea → 13-14

to place ads: to put notices or announcements in the newspaper → 90

to play it safe: to be on the safe side, to be out of harm's way, to take no chances, to stay out of danger, to take no risk → 125, 127

to play out: to develop, to proceed, to progress, to advance, to ensue → 116

to pleasantly surprise someone: to delightfully astonish or astound someone → 78

to pocket: to rake in, to gather in, to earn, to pull in, to accumulate → 47-48

to pool: to combine, to bundle, to merge, to group → 70

to possess: to be the owner of, to hold, to take into possession, to have, to enjoy → 135

to postpone: to put off, to delay, to rearrange, to reschedule, to defer → 49, 51, 95-96

to prefer: to favour, to choose, to select, to pick, to like better → 90

to press on: to continue to pursue, to broach the subject again, to push on → 101

to pretend not to be there: to feign or simulate that one is not present → 113

to prevail: to be in existence, prevalent, or current → 117, 123

to prevent: to put a stop to, to inhibit, to stave off, to ward off, to block, to thwart, to avoid → 35, 79, 81

to prevent something: to stop or avoid something → 81

to probe deeper into something: to get closer to the core of something → 74

to proceed: to go on, to carry on, to continue → 24, 40, 42, 95, 116, 138

to progress: to develop, to advance, to proceed, to move forwards → 21, 24, 116

to promise: to guarantee, to assure, to pledge, to give one's word to → 38, 42

to prompt: to cause, to induce, to incite, to impel, to encourage, to provoke, to motivate, to impel, to persuade, to tempt → 16, 18, 38, 65, 67, 69, 78, 86-87, 90

to prompt someone to do something: to cause, induce, or encourage someone to do something → 90

to prospect: to look or search for new customers → 88-89

to prove: to show, to verify, to confirm, to demonstrate, to attest → 45, 76, 127, 135

to prove someone right: to show that someone is absolutely correct → 45

to provide: to give, to offer, to present, to yield, to impart → 52, 100, 110, 118

to provoke: to evoke, to cause, to give rise to, to elicit, to induce → 18, 25, 90, 99, 124

to provoke protest: to cause, bring about, trigger, or give rise to objection → 90

to push for cost-saving measures: to enforce a cost-cutting or belt-tightening course of action → 113

to push someone to do something: to impel, goad, induce, or exhort someone to do something → 110

to put discussion of price on the backburner: to not talk about the costs right away → 24

to put one's foot in one's mouth: to drop a brick, to drop a clanger, to put one's foot in it → 13

to put pressure on someone: to coerce, bully, intimidate, or harass someone → 20

to put someone under pressure: to put the screws on or hassle someone → 110

to put the screws to someone: to apply pressure or leverage on someone → 34

to question one's assumption: to examine one's theory, hypothesis, or guess → 18

to quote: to cite, to refer to, to mention, to make reference to, to give, to name → 9, 15, 27, 35

to raise awareness: to increase → 74

to raise someone's anticipation: to boost someone's joyful expectancy → 104

to raise: to advance, to augment, to elevate, to heighten, to improve, to increase → 45, 55, 71, 73-74, 104

to rank: to position, to put in a specific order, to categorise, to classify → 60, 157

to rank among: to belong to the group of, to fit within the circle of → 60

to rate: to regard, to esteem, to value → 114

to reap: to harvest, to bring in, to take in → 141

to reassess: to re-examine, to re-evaluate, to reconsider, to have another look at → 105

to reassure someone: to set someone's mind at rest → 130

to recharge: to refresh, to revitalise, to revive → 132

to reckon: to be of the opinion, to believe, to suppose, to surmise, to deem → 155

to reckon with: to deal with, to handle, to contend with, to face → 155

to recognise: to identify, to make out, to spot, to detect, to pinpoint, to put the finger on → 7, 19, 41, 48, 82, 85, 95, 122, 137

to reconsider: to rethink, to go back over, to re-evaluate, to reassess, to have second thoughts about → 28, 101, 105

to re-evaluate: to re-examine, to re-assess, to have another look at → 97, 99, 105

to re-examine: to reconsider, to reassess, to re-evaluate, to check again → 99, 104-105

to refer to: to mention, to bring up, to talk about, to speak of → 9, 15

to refute: to disprove, to counter, to contest, to rebut → 18, 126, 128

to regard: to consider, to think of, to deem, to look upon, to view, to see → 101

to regret: to be unhappy with, to be remorseful about, to feel sorry about → 110

to reinforce: to strengthen, to fortify, to give a boost to, to bolster → 121

to release: to give the green light to, to make available → 46

to rely on: to bank on, to trust in, to count on, to bet on → 155

to remain: to stay, to keep on being, to continue to be → 28, 46, 128-130, 144

to remain in charge of: to stay in control or in command of → 34, 78

to remain matter-of-fact: to stay factual, down to earth, or unemotional → 46

to remain unfazed: to stay unflappable, to be in complete control → 129-130

to remain unflappable: to stay in control, composed, level-headed, self-possessed, or collected → 28

to remain unresponsive to something: to stay indifferent or impassive to something → 128

to reply: to respond, to answer back → 13

to require: to demand, to necessitate, to entail, to involve → 9, 104, 120

to resolve the issue: to work out or sort out the problem → 40, 42

to resort to: to fall back on, to turn to, to make use of, to bring into play → 13

to respond to: to react or act in response to, to take action → 7, 13, 21, 25

to respond to something: to react in response or acknowledge something → 7, 21

to restrain oneself: contain, or hinder oneself, to hold oneself back, to keep oneself in check → 146

to retain: to keep, to keep hold of, to hold on to, to preserve, to keep possession of → 46, 110

to revamp: to overhaul, to recondition, to fix up, to give a face-lift to → 152

to reveal: to impart, to communicate, to disclose, to divulge, to show, to uncover, to bring to light → 41, 114, 121, 135, 152

to review: to re-examine, to reassess, to have another look at, to make another study of → 28

to revise: to reconsider, to review → 28

to rid someone of something: to free, liberate, unburden, or relieve someone of something → 75

to rouse: to stir up, to incite, to awaken, to provoke, to evoke → 25

to run the gauntlet: being critically and unsympathetically observed by a group of people → 127

to scare: to alarm, to make nervous, to intimidate, to shock → 27, 29

to schedule an appointment: to set a date for a visit, to arrange a meeting → 21, 50, 88

to score with someone: to make an impression or be a hit with someone → 138

to scrutinise: to examine, to analyse, to inspect, to go over, to peruse → 153

to secure: to acquire, to obtain, to get, to come by, to get hold of, to assure. to ensure. to promise, to give surety to → 38, 58, 153

to see to it: to take care, to arrange, to organise, to be responsible → 59

to seek out: to try to find, to hunt for, to pursue, to be after → 152

to seize: to grab, to take hold of, to take advantage of, to grab hold of, to get hold of → 7, 95

to sense: to get the impression, to have a feeling, to perceive → 64, 67, 85, 114, 125

to serve as: to act as, to function as, to do duty as, to do the work of → 9, 46, 48, 59

to serve as an extension of something: to function or act as an addition or adjunct to something → 48

to set a precedent: to become the standard or guide → 48

to set one's sights on: to aim at, to aspire to, to strive toward, to work toward → 70

to set up: to establish, to create, to get going, to start, to institute, to produce, to achieve, to pull off, to bring into being, to initiate → 51, 144

to set up appointments: to arrange, plan, or organise visits with customers → 51

to settle into one's new job: to make oneself acquainted or familiarise oneself with one's new work → 146

to share: to communicate, to let somebody in on, to reveal, to disclose, to impart, to divide up, to split → 133, 135

to single out: to separate out, to set apart, to pick, to choose, to decide on → 157

to snub: to affront, to offend, to upset, to insult, to slight → 122, 124

to sound out: to investigate, to explore, to examine, to probe → 94, 96

to speed up: to accelerate, to hurry up → 42

to spoil: to ruin, to mess up, to destroy → 13, 25

to squint: to narrow one's eyes, to look askance → 18

to steer: to guide, to manoeuvre, to lead, to direct, to navigate → 14, 51, 83, 101

to strengthen: to make stronger, to give strength to, to fortify, to give a boost to → 38

to struggle with something: to try to come to grips or deal with something → 113

to subdivide: to classify, to sort, to arrange, to order, to categorise → 25

to submit: to present, to put forward, to proffer, to hand in, to propose, to set forth → 100

to suffer: to experience, to undergo, to go through, to endure → 86

to suffice: to meet the requirements, to be sufficient, adequate or enough, to satisfy the demands → 14

to supervise: to manage, to direct, to control, to take charge of → 70

to surround: to encircle, to enfold, to ring, to gird → 27-29

to sustain: to hold, to maintain, to uphold, to preserve → 46

to sweat the small stuff: to pay attention to details or fine points → 19

to tackle: to busy oneself with, to apply oneself to, to take on, to get to work at → 104

to tailor to: to adapt, modify, or adjust to → 100

to take action: to do something, to proceed, to take steps, to get busy, to react → 138

to take advantage of something: to make the most of, make use of, or cash in on something, to profit from, cash in on, or make the most of something → 105

to take apart: to disassemble, to take to pieces, to take to bits → 27, 29

to take calculated steps: to take deliberate, purposeful, or planned measures → 155

to take into consideration: to bear in mind, to take into account, to be mindful or heedful of, to remember, to pay regard or heed to → 42, 93, 99-100

to take someone to task: to confront, give a talking-to, rebuke, or reprimand someone → 41

to take something seriously: to not take something frivolously or flippantly → 21

to tempt: to allure, to attract, to entice, to persuade, to lure → 67

to tense up: to feel under pressure, nervous, keyed-up, or strained → 28

to throw in the towel: to resign, to quit, to give up, to walk away, to capitulate → 116

to throw someone off: to take someone unawares or by surprise → 96

to tie someone to something: to bind or commit someone to something, to make someone stay loyal to something → 58

to tip the scales: to have a major influence on the outcome of a situation → 134-135

to totter: to be unstable or unsteady → 26, 28

to treat: to act or behave towards, to deal with, to handle → 41, 123, 134-135

to treat oneself to something: to indulge, spoil, or pamper oneself → 135

to trigger: to activate, to set off, to generate, to prompt, to elicit, to cause, to bring about → 69, 78, 86, 113

to trust: to believe, to expect, to hope → 66, 78, 133, 137

to turn out to be true: to happen to be correct, to end up being accurate → 101

to turn special attention to: to direct particular awareness toward → 67

to underline: to underscore, to emphasise, to highlight → 45, 69, 82, 121, 155

to utilise: to make use of, to employ, to resort to, to take advantage of, to use, to put to use, to employ, to handle → 21, 135

to verify: to make sure, to ensure, to confirm → 67, 121, 127

to view: to regard, to think about, to feel about, to perceive, to deem → 59, 80-81, 156

to vindicate oneself: to justify or defend oneself → 86

to voice: to put in words, to express, to give utterance to, to articulate, to communicate → 96

to weigh every word: to judge, assess, or contemplate each remark → 126

to what extent: to what degree, amount, level, or point → 150

to win over: to bring around, to persuade, to prevail upon, to influence → 24, 58, 76, 122-123, 153

to witness: to see, to observe, to watch → 145

to woo someone: to court, pursue, or seek to win someone → 132

to yearn for something: to desire, long for, crave, or hunger for something → 75

toll-free: free of charge, at no cost, without charge → 69

tool: instrument, resource, vehicle, catalyst, channel, mean → 80

topics: subjects, themes, things to talk about → 8-9, 12

touchstone: criterion, yardstick, benchmark, acid test, standard → 69-70

trace: bit, touch, hint, drop → 54, 56

transition: change, changeover, move, switch, shift, conversion → 6-7, 9-10, 20, 109-110

trap: pifall, snare, stumbling block, catch, snare, net, deception → 13, 130

trickiest: most complicated, problematic, awkward, difficult, precarious → 21, 24

trusted: familiar, close, trustworthy, reliable → 142-143

trusting: trustful, reliable, dependable → 147, 150

trustworthy: dependable, reliable → 12, 14, 17, 19, 134, 143, 155

turning point: crossroads, critical period, decisive point → 142-143

turnover: gross revenue, volume of business → 120-121

two-digit: any number between 10 and 99 → 77-78

ultimately: in the end, eventually, finally → 26, 32, 40-42, 65

under the direction of: headed, led, run, or managed by → 64, 66

underrated: undervalued, underestimated, not done justice to, rated too low → 149, 152

unintentionally: accidentally, inadvertently, not deliberately, unintended, by accident, by chance, involuntarily → 6-7, 128, 130

unnoticed: unobserved, unseen, without being seen → 136

unsatisfactory: unacceptable, substandard, not up to scratch, poor → 83, 85

unserviceable: useless, worthless, inadequate, ineffective → 112, 114

unspoken: undeclared, unsaid, unexpressed, not spelled out → 111, 113

upbeat fashion: optimistic, positive, confident, or cheerful way → 11, 13

uppermost: primary, main, principal, greatest, most important → 36, 50-51

upset: annoyed, angry, irritated, exasperated, aggravated → 42, 124

urgency: importance, necessity, top priority, exigency, imperativeness → 84, 86

utility costs: expenses for electricity, gas, water → 112, 114

utilization: use, usage, handling → 126-127

vain: conceited, narcissistic, self-admiring, self-important, big-headed → 12, 14, 79, 81, 95-96

valued: esteemed, highly regarded, respected, cherished, treasured → 32, 59, 133, 136, 154

varied: diverse, assorted, miscellaneous, diversified, wide-ranging, different → 40, 42, 48, 77

variety of couplings: assortment or a selection of mechanical devices that join or connect two parts → 50, 52

various: different, diverse, assorted, miscellaneous, choice of, numerous, many, a number of → 77-79, 149

vehicle owner: registered or recorded keeper → 67

vicinity: surrounding area, neighbourhood, environs → 6-7

virtually: almost, nearly, practically, in effect, as good as, effectively, next to, nearly, essentially → 122, 124

vital: very important, critical, imperative, essential, crucial, central → 46, 91-92, 135, 141, 154

vividly: graphically, clearly, lively, → 22, 25

wage: salary, earnings, income, take-home pay, remuneration → 114

walk on a tightrope: high-wire act, razor-edge affair → 73, 75

waste disposal: removal of refuse os waste → 66, 68

wasted: used up, squandered, dissipated → 91, 93

way out: possibility for escape → 9

weaker: less effective or powerful → 22, 24

well-established: well-founded, well-grounded, well-substantiated → 156-157

well-meaning: kind, benevolent, caring → 26, 28

what became of something: what happened to or what was the outcome of something → 51

what is at your disposal: what you already have available or on hand → 70

when in doubt: when undecided, uncertain, unsure, or doubtful → 116

which can be accessed: which can be opened, retrieved, logged on to, or read → 49, 51

with regard to: concerning, about, on the subject or matter of, as regards → 61

within the realm: within the framework, scheme, system, area, or field → 120-121

without delay: immediately, right away, at once, straight away, promptly, quickly, fast, expeditiously → 144-145

without noticing: devoid of becoming aware, perceiving, detecting, or observing → 146, 148

worrier: person who is concerned that something bad might happen → 128, 130

worry: concern, anxiety, trouble, apprehension, care → 45, 74-75, 85, 116, 135, 137

wrongdoing: professional misconduct, mistake, unprofessional behaviour → 91, 93

yield: earnings, income, returns, profit, proceeds, revenue → 100

your counterpart: person across from or facing you → 15, 17

MANAGEMENT

INFORMÁTICA

CULTURA GENERAL

RELACIONES

ESPIRITUALIDAD

SALUD